American Automobilia

An Illustrated History and Price Guide

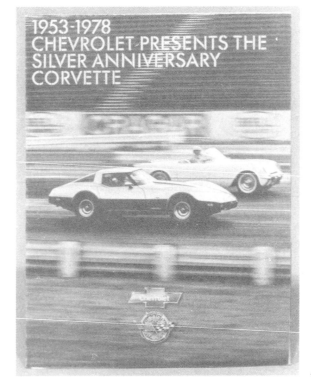

1953-1978
CHEVROLET PRESENTS THE
SILVER ANNIVERSARY
CORVETTE

FAYE
1956

American Automobilia

An Illustrated History
and Price Guide

Jim & Nancy Schaut

WALLACE-HOMESTEAD

BOOK COMPANY

Radnor, Pennsylvania

Copyright © 1994 by Jim and Nancy Schaut

All Rights Reserved

Published in Radnor, Pennsylvania 19089, by Wallace-Homestead,
a division of Chilton Book Company

Designed by Adrianne Onderdonk Dudden
Manufactured in the United States of America

Library of Congress Cataloging-in-Publication Data

Schaut, Jim.
    American automobilia : an illustrated history and price
guide / Jim and Nancy Schaut.
      p.   cm.
    Includes bibliographical reference and index.
    ISBN 0-87069-688-2
    1. Automobiles — Collectibles — United States — Catalogs.
2. Automobiles — Equipment and supplies — Collectors and collecting —
United States — Catalogs. I. Schaut, Nancy. II. Title.
TL7.U6S33 1994   93-25194
                                                        CIP

1 2 3 4 5 6 7 8 9   3 2 1 0 9 8 7 6 5 4

Contents

American Automobilia

An Illustrated History and Price Guide

Introduction

Automobilia refers to the widely varied field of automotive-related memorabilia, but it is much too broad a subject to be defined with a single word. Automobilia is, in fact, a little bit of everything. The cars themselves and their hard parts, such as fenders, hoods, doors, and bumpers, are not usually considered automobilia. Rather, it is accessories and decorative items, such as curb feelers, radiator mascots, and hubcaps, that are collected.

Some people collect vintage cars, stockpiling one after another until their neighbors' tolerance to the clutter wears thin. Others prefer the more subtle hobby of collecting automobilia. An accumulation of dealer advertising signs, promotional model cars, or complimentary oil company maps takes up far less room and is less offensive to friends and family than the rusting hulk of an Edsel station wagon in the driveway.

Our love of the automobile and the gathering of all things auto-related began when modern man first put engine to buggy and found he could do very nicely without the horse. Since the introduction of this horseless carriage to North America near the end of the nineteenth century, Americans have been fascinated with all things automotive. American life came to revolve around the automobile. No other country has devoted so much time, work, retail space, magazine pages, and media airtime to the motorcar. We love our cars!

Steam power preceded gasoline by some time. In France, Cugnot attempted to move military equipment with steam-powered vehicles as early as 1770. In the United States, Sylvester Roper of Roxbury, Massachusetts, was building and selling steam buggies in the 1860s. Decades ahead of his time, Roper is often credited with the development of the motorcycle, as his company also manufactured a steam-powered velocipede. The name Stanley is most commonly identified with American steam vehicles. Twin brothers

Francis and Freeland Stanley built their first automobile in 1896. This automobile accomplished many feats that gas-powered vehicles of the era could not, including a climb to the peak of New England's highest mountain. As a result of these publicity stunts, the Stanley Steamer was in great demand. The brothers went into full production, selling two hundred cars in 1899 and continuing until the mid-1920s.

Electric cars, touted by automakers today as the answer to the world's pollution problems, are nothing new. In 1839, Scotty Anderson of Aberdeen, Scotland, built an electric car. By 1898, the Electric Vehicle Company of Hartford, Connecticut, was manufacturing the Columbia electric car. Riker of New Jersey got its three-wheeler into production the same year. The public loved the electric automobiles because they were so smooth and quiet to operate.

The Duryea brothers are usually given credit for manufacturing the first gasoline-powered American car. Frank and Charles, working out of their bicycle shop, produced their first Duryea in 1893, although the two-cylinder 1894 model was more successful. Frank, driving the second Duryea, won the *Chicago Times–Herald* round-trip auto race from Chicago to Evanston on Thanksgiving Day in 1895. Winning over some of the more sophisticated European machines of the day was quite a triumph for the little American machine. The Duryeas were the first to sell a gas-powered vehicle in the United States and the first to export an American-made, gasoline-powered automobile for sale.

About the same time, hundreds of other Americans were building their own version of the motorcar in their backyards and barns. These shade-tree mechanics, in the true American spirit of "do it yourself," wanted to cheaply build an automobile for their own use. In fact, as early as 1901, a handyman could send for a mail-order kit for a one-cylinder automobile.

Building a car on your own was simply a matter of economics. In the early days of motorcar development, automobiles were so costly to build by hand that only the very rich could afford such toys. This held true until lower-priced, commercially produced models, such as the Oldsmobile and Henry Ford's Model T, came on the market. However, these seemingly low-priced automobiles still required a significant investment. Buying a basic Model T took the better part of a year's salary from most blue-collar and farm families.

The automobile was a great liberator of women. Oldsmobile even targeted the woman driver in some of its earliest advertising. Women drivers were more common in those first days of the motorcar than you might think. In 1899, Mrs. John Phillips of Chicago became the first woman to be issued a driver's license, long before many men had done so. In 1909, Mrs. John Ramsey and three women friends traveled from New York to San Francisco in a Maxwell car. The trip took fifty-three days! The accomplishments of today's women drivers pale in comparison with the hardships suffered by these four women motoring coast to coast on unmarked roads that were little more than cattle trails.

By the 1920s, American automakers overwhelmingly favored the gasoline engine. No new electric or steam-powered automobiles were introduced at the National Automobile Show of 1924. This was a decade of change in the United States and the auto industry was no exception. Henry Ford closed out production of his successful Model T after selling fifteen million and introduced the Model A. Ford also astounded the public by raising the pay of the average Ford factory worker to $7 per day!

The Great Depression of the 1930s changed the lives of many Americans, especially the many small, independent automakers who were forced out of business by slumping sales. More than five million automobiles were sold in 1929 before the October crash but less than one-half that number were sold in 1930. Desperate automakers tried to pump up slumping sales by offering a bounty on old cars. It is appalling to today's collectors, but from 1931 to 1933, hundreds of thousands of "outdated" automobiles were sent to the crusher so that they could not be resold as used vehicles. Sound familiar? Talk about history repeating itself; this is the same concept that some legislators are proposing today.

Even though World War II was worsening in Europe, American carmakers were reluctant to think about arms manufacture. Sales were finally showing recovery from the depression, and in 1941, General Motors enjoyed its highest net income in corporate history. Pearl Harbor, of course, changed the attitude of the automakers, who retooled as quickly as possible for their World War II manufacturing efforts. The last civilian automobiles rolled off the assembly lines early in 1942. Wartime advertising kept the automakers' names in the minds of the American public while touting their contributions to the war effort. Buick's slogan was "When better automobiles are built again, Buick will build them."

In the years after World War II, cars were hot sellers. Buyers flooded the showrooms to purchase even leftover 1942 models. Automakers went into full peacetime production. With the pent-up demand and an increasingly mobile American public, automobile companies quickly became the richest corporations in the United States.

As pre–World War II memorabilia becomes harder to find, dealer promotional items from this very active postwar era increase in popularity. Those little "Thank You" gifts, such as toy model cars, calendars, matchbooks, perfumes, umbrellas, pinback buttons, and rules and sales literature, were offered every time a customer walked into a showroom or took a new model out for a test drive. The huge amount of automobilia from the 1950s and 1960s is still relatively easy to find and is as popular with today's collectors as are the vehicles of the day.

In the 1970s, automobile companies met with new obstacles in the form of government regulations on air pollution. Compliance, it was claimed, was the sole cause of soaring automobile prices. Slumping sales forced automakers to cut advertising budgets, and fewer free gifts were offered to the casual tire kicker. Sales brochures were still available but were not as detailed or as colorful.

Today, automakers are faced with intense competition from foreign carmakers and are trying to revive consumer interest in American automobiles. They are attacking our senses with nostalgic advertising, with promises of both performance and economy, and with sportier looks even in four-door sedans. Limited-production vehicles, such as the Corvette ZR-1 and Chrysler's Viper, have recaptured the imagination of the consumer. Dealers are once again offering promotional models, license plate frames, bumper stickers, T-shirts, jackets, banks, and other advertising. This readily available modern advertising will someday become collectible. An example is the mass-produced items offered by Chevrolet dealers bearing their current "Heartbeat of America" logo. This is one of the most popular and long-running advertising slogans since "There's a Ford in your future" and is already being collected by Chevrolet enthusiasts.

Nowhere is the old axiom "There's nothing new under the sun" more appropriate than in the automotive industry. Each new and improved model sports a feature that the manufacturer claims is innovative but that is actually recycled from an earlier model. Turn signals were standard on the 1921 Leland Lincoln. Four-wheel, independent suspension was offered in the 1922 Lancia. Twin overhead cams were available in the 1912 Peugot. Two-tone paint combinations, like the pink and gray so popular in the 1950s, was nothing new. The 1915 Packard came with a two-color paint scheme.

When we first decided to write this book on collecting automobilia, our first thoughts were of the thousands of automobile hobbyists who love old cars and who collect anything and everything pertaining to them. If it has a picture of an automobile on it, they want it. Realizing that all old-car hobbyists are pack rats at heart and that many of us cannot afford a signed Peter Helck painting or a Lalique radiator mascot, we have tried to include a lot of the less expensive collectibles, items that can still be purchased for around $20. This enables the average person to build a nice collection of quality items with a minimal investment. There is a lot of potentially collectible automobilia that can be had for just a few dollars today. Chrome side emblems, such as the Mustang horse, cardboard oilcan banks, oil company maps, dealer sales brochures, and tire-shaped key chains are still very reasonably priced.

Automobilia collecting has changed drastically in recent years. Increased demand has caused prices to soar on the more unusual items. Prices fluctuate from one part of the country to another. We hope that this guide will inform collectors as well as help standardize prices throughout the hobby industry.

Automobile-related collectibles can be found everywhere and anywhere. Aunt Ethel may still have the raincoat, handbag, and umbrella she got in 1955 when she bought that new Dodge La Femme. That strange-looking cube-shaped yardstick in Grandpa's garage may be the one his father got to measure the gasoline level in the tank of his Model T. Modern improvements like the gas gauge eliminated the need to carry this stick, relegating it to obsolescence and, eventually, collectibility.

Automobilia can be almost anything—a ceramic Avon bottle, a club newsletter, a race program, a Glidden tour postcard, an old road map, a sales brochure for the 1959 Edsel, or a promotional model of the Dodge Viper. It can be old or fairly modern. Most treasured are the few items relating to automobiles manufactured before 1900. It can be fairly common, though, like the heavy restaurant-grade stoneware used in employee cafeterias or something really special, like the porcelain pieces in the Royal Doulton "The Motorist" series.

Vintage clothing cannot be overlooked as an element of the hobby. The duster, hat, and goggles so necessary to driver and passengers in open touring cars are often worn by today's auto enthusiasts when they display their vintage automobiles or participate in a touring event. Just as drivers of 1950s cars like to dress in rolled-up jeans and slick their hair back into a ducktail, so do owners of early automobiles love to dress in the styles of that era; whether the Gay Nineties or flappers, it's all part of the fun of the hobby.

Although automobile parts meets and antiques shows are great places to find automotive collectibles, they can also be found at local auctions, swap meets, and garage sales. There are also new shops opening all over the country that specialize in automotive toys, art, and collectibles.

Old-car ownership is on the rise. Interest in driving and restoring old cars shows no signs of tapering off, and the hobby of collecting automobilia is growing by leaps and bounds.

If you long for the sight of a friendly face in a world that seems hostile and sometimes violent, just drive an old car. Join a car club, attend your local automotive events, and get to know these special folks. Drive your old car and people you don't even know will wave and give you a hearty "thumbs up" sign. As a rule, old-car people are among the friendliest and most helpful you'll ever come across. Enjoy the hobby!

State of the Market

Americans love their old cars. Even President Bill Clinton drives a 1966 Mustang convertible. The preservation, restoration, historical research, and display of collector vehicles is a hobby that pumps millions of dollars into the U.S. economy each year. The market for auto-related collectibles, from banks to T-shirts, is strong.

Such demand often causes prices to soar, as in the case of the tiny figural salt and pepper sets fashioned after the gas pumps of the 1950s. Unusual oil company logos on these cheaply made service station premiums were in demand. Prices soared to more than $100 several years ago, thanks to a steady stream of collectors looking for them. These high prices quickly cooled what had been a "hot" market as hobbyists looked for something less trendy and less expensive to collect. Today, prices of these salt and pepper sets are back to their 1990 levels and demand has slowed. It is hard to sell a set unless it is very rare or very reasonably priced.

As long as there is a demand for automotive-related collectibles, prices will continue to increase. Recent auction results, catalogs, and dealer sales lists confirm that prices of unusual automobilia have gone up as much as 50 percent over the past year. At the same time, automobilia in excellent to mint condition is scarce.

We want to give the collector and automobile hobbyist some information that may help them to identify their automobilia and accurately determine the condition and age of their collectibles. Our price lists following the text of each chapter will give a ballpark figure for each item. There will be some who feel our prices are too high or too low. However, we have combined our experiences in selling automobilia with that of other enthusiasts and with auction reports and advertisements in hobby publications to establish a price that is representative of a national average.

Regional differences and preferences make

a big difference in pricing. For example, a ready market for NASCAR—National Association of Stock Car Auto Racing—collectibles exists in the Southeast while memorabilia from the Pep Boys automotive accessory stores enjoys a strong following on the West Coast.

Condition is the most important factor to consider when purchasing any collectible. Mint items with their original box (MIB) or packaging will command considerably higher prices than items showing wear or abuse, as will items in very good (vg) condition. Automobile-related collectibles are often described as NOS, meaning "New Old Stock." This term usually applies to an unused, original item. Some additional abbreviations you can expect to see in the listings besides MIB, NOS, and vg are 10KGF (ten carat gold filled) and 1# (one pound). It is best to steer away from any automobilia that is damaged or has missing parts. Save your money for the best possible examples you can afford. It is better to have a few excellent pieces in your collection than a shelf full of battered, bruised, and rusted automotive collectibles. Of course, intent makes a difference. If you want an old wooden spoked rim to use as a planter in the front yard, condition is not as important as it would be if you wanted rims to put on your restored horseless carriage. Of course, you would not pay as much for a rusted rim to use as a yard decoration. As in most collecting, common sense prevails.

A shortage of items, whether real or contrived, can also cause a sharp rise in prices. Reproductions will also cause fluctuation in market values. It is not unusual for the value of an original item to decrease when a reproduction becomes available. Be an informed collector. If an item looks brand new and is unusually low priced, odds are good that it is a remake. Original dates of manufacture and copyright information are often copied as well.

A lot of memorabilia reminiscent of the 1950s and 1960s is being reproduced, from poodle skirts and saddle shoes to fuzzy dice, drive-in speakers, and carhop trays. These trinkets are fun to display with your vintage automobile at car shows, but keep in mind that they are new and pay accordingly.

Very little authentic memorabilia has survived since the appearance of the motorcar in the United States late in the nineteenth century. Many of the auto-related antiques that still exist from this era are already in museums or private collections. Original artwork is sometimes offered for sale at auction. In general, paintings seem to have been well cared for and are usually offered for sale in very good condition. On occasion, a stray piece of Royal Doulton's turn-of-the-century "The Motor" series will turn up at an estate sale. Check all ceramics carefully, looking for chips, cracks, and evidence of repairs.

Any memorabilia advertising the prestigious motorcars of the 1920s and 1930s, such as Auburn, Cord, Duesenberg, or Packard, is always in demand, although new collectors seem to be leaning toward memorabilia of the 1950s and 1960s cars. Just as collectors nearing retirement age reminisce about their family's Model A, so baby boomers love the cars that their moms and dads drove. GI Joes, metal lunch pails, and Barbie dolls are right up there with the 1955 Chevrolets and Mustangs on every boomer's wish list. Much memorabilia of this era is still readily available and at comparatively reasonable prices.

While Fords and Chevrolets seem most popular with collectors, look for increased interest in the Chrysler Corporation muscle cars of the 1960s, especially the Plymouth Superbird. Advertising, promotional models, factory-issued toys and games, and drag racing memorabilia pertaining to its famous hemi engine is already sought after. These Mopars virtually ruled the racing scene at that time, and there are enough toys, magazines, race programs, and photographs available to satisfy the most die-hard racing memorabilia collector.

A "sleeper," or somewhat overlooked, area of muscle car collecting is memorabilia from the low-production American Motors Company (AMC) cars of that era — the Hurst Rambler Scrambler and the Rebel Machine are two rarely seen AMC factory muscle cars. Any advertising memorabilia from these cars is just plain hard to find. AMC never had an advertising budget large enough to enable its dealerships to keep up with the Big Three — Ford, General Motors (GM), and Chrysler — so its promotional models, advertising giveaways, are all the more rare.

One of our favorite future collectibles is the Jeep. An offspring of World War II, this tough little four-wheel drive has at one time or another proudly worn the nameplate of some of the great old names in American automotive history — Willys, Kaiser, American Motors, and Chrysler. Changes in the Chrysler lineup have eliminated the full-size Wagoneer, a staple since 1963 and the rugged sire of today's luxurious "utility vehicles." So hang on to the Jeep advertising and collectibles!

The availability and popularity of automobilia goes hand in hand with the popularity of the marque, that is, the brand or make. There are more Chevrolet and Ford collectibles available and less Packard simply because more Chevrolet and Ford automobiles were sold. Everyone believes that the 1957 Chevrolet was the most popular car ever, but how many realize that Ford actually outsold Chevrolet in 1957? If such statistics fascinate you, try collecting literature. Written automotive history is a vast subject, containing many smaller areas of specialization — collecting owner's manuals, technical shop manuals, or dealer advertising postcards. Prices of literature continue to increase.

Here again, the most intense interest is in automobile racing literature. Auto racing has had several recent milestones: Richard Petty has retired from the NASCAR scene and Don ("Big Daddy") Garlitts has retired his dragster after a long and very successful career. Any racing memorabilia relating to these superstars will be collected for years to come.

Finding automobilia is not as difficult a task as finding affordable automobilia. Antiques stores, malls, and shows are often a great source of auto-related collectibles. Prices tend to be a bit lower than they are at specialized shows, such as automobile auctions, car shows, and swap meets. A prize piece of automotive history will sometimes turn up at garage sales or flea markets. Estate sales, especially those near large automobile company plants, offices, or other facilities, are good sources for company service pins, plant badges, desk sets, and the like. Given the popularity of transportation toys, it sometimes seems a miracle to find anything. The secret is to keep looking and to ask. You never know what might turn up if you ask the homeowner, sales manager, or auctioneer for automobile-related items.

Now, don't you have an urge to go out and buy something that you really like? Finding a duplicate of the first model your dad ever bought you, an advertisement for that 1953 Corvette you couldn't afford, a vinyl statue of the Michelin Man, or a chubby little Buddy Lee doll in a Texaco uniform would be a great beginning for your collection. There is a vast amount of automobilia and petroliana out there just waiting to be discovered by an old-car lover like yourself. It's a great time to be a collector. Happy hunting!

1

Advertising

Automobile advertising is the most often collected type of automobilia. Signs from dealerships, particularly from automakers such as Packard and Nash, who are no longer in business, are especially desirable. A large porcelain sign from an old dealership can easily set the hobbyist back a thousand dollars. The colorful neon signs commonly used in the 1950s and 1960s are also becoming popular with collectors.

Knowing some of the basic facts of automobile history helps the hobbyist determine the age and value of his or her collection. When automobile advertising memorabilia is dated or shows a likeness of the current model, it is relatively easy to date the item by identifying the year of the car itself. However, porcelain and metal signs that hung outdoors for many years are usually undated. Sometimes collectible automobilia must be dated by knowing when an automaker ceased production or when it utilized a certain logo or symbol. For instance, Packard advertising memorabilia will always date from the 1950s or earlier as the last Packard rolled off the assembly line in 1958.

When a date is lacking, look for a country of origin. Dealer giveaways for American cars were produced all over the globe—usually where it could be done most cheaply. Currently, the Chevrolet "Heartbeat of America" banks are made in China. Some of the older auto advertising was made in the United States, but much of the 1950s and 1960s memorabilia found will be marked "Japan" or "Hong Kong."

Automobile advertising has always been inventive and amusing. The manufacturers and local dealers wanted nothing less than for us to go about our daily business humming their advertising theme song: "Have you driven a Ford lately?" A diversity of logos, slogans, and celebrity spokespersons—some real, such as Dinah Shore, and some imaginary, such as Joe Isuzu—has made for some memorable moments in print, radio, and television advertising. Many times, ads or dealer handouts can be dated by the celebrity appearing in them. For example, actors Lorne Green, Dan Blocker, and Michael Landon were used in Chevrolet ads in the mid-sixties when that company sponsored "Bonanza." Sophie Tucker gave away new 1939 Chevrolets on her radio program. Most baby boomers remember Dinah Shore appearing on our tiny black-and-white television sets singing "See the USA in your Chevrolet." Wild and wacky advertising pitchmen like Joe Isuzu—He's lying—are nothing new to those of us who grew up with that mad scientist, Dr. Oldsmobile. Dodge gave us the perky but "Mean Mary Jean" and Joe Higgins, the redneck sheriff.

One of the best remembered advertising campaigns ever is the slogan, "There's a Ford in your Future." For years after World War II, much Ford advertising contained this slogan and the famous crystal ball with a new model Ford within. During this time, many Ford dealers had a large crystal ball in their showrooms displaying several promotional model cars representing the new models. That display would be a great addition to any collection of dealer advertising. Chevrolet's later campaign touting baseball, hot dogs, apple pie, and Chevrolet appealed to our patriotism. Dodge dealers appealed to our sense of right and wrong when they appeared as the "good guys" with the white hats. Currently, the Chevrolet "Heartbeat of America" campaign is producing thousands of bits of potentially collectible automobilia all over the world.

The most common dealer advertising collectibles are the thousands of small customer handouts, such as paper plates, rulers, playing cards, promotional model cars, and children's toys. From baseballs to yo-yos, including calendars, perfume, plastic rain hats, window

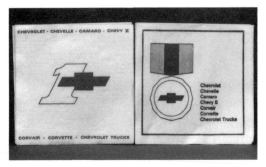

Chevrolet napkins, 1960s, lists all models, $3 each.

Pinto/Coca-Cola cooler, $15.

scrapers, showroom banners, desk ornaments and lights, dealer premiums are collected along with the more rare dealer-issued items, such as salesmen's personalized desk ornaments and awards, factory photos and correspondence, and mechanics' service pins. All automobilia is desirable to collectors, but quality is more important than quantity. A salesman's service pin, commemorating twenty-five years with a dealership and that is ten karat gold with a diamond chip, will have a much higher value than a pinback button commemorating a specific sales campaign.

You always hear stories about people stopping at dealerships in remote small towns and buying old salesmen's sample books, porcelain signs, and NOS accessories in their factory boxes. The price is always said to be a steal. While some older dealerships may still be using their vintage signs, these bargains are much less common than you might be led to think. However, don't think bargains are not out there. There are sleepers; a tremendous amount of automobile-related collectibles may be out there in Uncle Joe's basement or in Granny's attic, just waiting for you to find it. Talk to your friends and neighbors. Ask questions; a neighbor's father or grandfather may have retired from a Chevrolet plant or a Ford dealership. Former autoworkers probably have quite a bit of interesting automobilia stored away. Even if they don't, they have memories they will usually be happy to share with you. This oral automotive history, from stories of pranks on the assembly line to insider gossip about managerial tugs-of-war, is priceless.

Some automobile collectibles have even been rescued from the trash heap by alert hobbyists. In one case, a man was razing an old shed on his property and discovered some tin signs from an old dealership that had been used to patch the roof.

Many of the smaller automobile advertising signs are being reproduced at this time. Most reputable dealers will identify a reproduction sign as such, but a few try to age such signs and pass them off as originals. Reproduction tin signs are a thinner gauge metal than the originals, but the porcelain reproductions are well done and a little harder to detect. Reproduction signs, purchased with full knowledge that they are new, can provide a colorful display among a collection of original automobilia.

Finding dealer advertising requires a bit of detective work. You must do some research on the marque you are interested in collecting. Find out when the dealers used a certain logo, when they changed colors on

Mopar Silicone Auto Cleaner Tin, 1960s, $20.

their signs, or when that dealership went out of business. These answers will help you to date and price any dealer advertising you may have an interest in.

Above all, ask. There is nothing old-car lovers like to do better than talk! They are generous in sharing information. At swap meets, query the vendors — "Ya got any DeSoto stuff?" They may, even if they don't have any out on display. No one has the space to haul and display everything in his or her collection or inventory.

In the past one hundred plus years of motoring in the United States, millions of pieces of automobile dealer advertising have found their way into the hands of the American public. Now it's up to you, the auto enthusiast, to find them and preserve them for future generations. The automobile is often blamed for many of the problems facing our country. Through collecting automobilia, it is possible to see the many positive contributions that the horseless carriage has made through the years.

Ashtray

Aluminum, embossed, Fisher Body–GM 75th Anniversary, $10

Ceramic, Walter Schatt, Willys distributor, Rookwood Pottery, $90

Copper, Cadillac Motor Car Division, 1948, large shield emblem in center, $35

Copper, Chrysler Corporation, 1933, souvenir from the World's Fair, Chicago, Century of Progress theme, MIB, $40

Glass, 4″ diameter, painted center reads "Buick, 1903–53," $15

Badge, brass, Chevrolet Baltimore Plant Dedication, blue cloisonné bow tie, place for name, dated April 9, 1935, $100

Bank

Cardboard, 1952 Chevrolet automobile printed on one side, 1952 truck on the other, $20

Metal, promotional model of a 1952 Cadillac four-door sedan, painted light blue, cast by Banthrico, $100

Metal globe, reads "Best Buick yet," 1930s, $75

Tin, Dodge, oil barrel shape, reads "Switch to Dodge and Save Money," 1930s era, $40

Banner, showroom, "New 1939 Pontiac," purple silk with gold fringe, colors slightly faded from the sun, $50

Bell, hand held, "I'm ringing the bell with the Pontiac," $30

Belt Buckle, embossed Model T, reads "Henry Ford, Detroit, Model T Record Year," a reissue, $10

Bird, Plastic bird with wings spread, advertising figure introducing the Ford Falcon in 1960, $75

Blotter

Calendar, 1932, Oregon auto dealer, $15

Dodge panel truck, 1925, mint unused, Massachusetts dealer, $25

Johengen garage, Willys-Knight, Overland and Whippet specialist, Buffalo, New York, $30

Board Game, Drag Racing Game, a mail-order premium available through Chrysler-Plymouth dealers, 1960s, $75

Bullet Pencil, Willys-Knight, gift from Iowa dealer, $15

Buzzard, plush, mascot, Arizona Chevrolet dealer, $10

Camera, given by Chevrolet dealers in the mid-1970s after a test drive in a Vega, new in the box, $15

Can Opener, white pearl handle, red plastic bullet in one end, old-style bottle opener at the other, Illinois Chevrolet dealer, $10

Candy Dish

Glass with lid, reads "Pontiac builds fleet excitement," $10

Sterling, "1966 Ford 300-500 Club," $45

Checkbook Cover, white vinyl, gold letters and Chevrolet "bow tie" logo, Wisconsin Chevrolet dealer, $5

Clicker, child's toy, green/yellow, reads "Plymouth Cricket," $5

Clock, neon, 1950s Oldsmobile logo, showroom display item, $100

Coasters, 4″ square, blue plastic, 1960s, Cadillac dealer, set of four, $5

Coffee Mugs, white ceramic, red and blue lettering, a bicentennial premium from an Illinois Chevrolet dealer, $10

Cuff Links

Dodge Super Bee, matching tie bar, $50

New Departure Hyatt Bearings, Division of General Motors, tiny bearing mounted on flat cuff link, $35

Desk Calendar

Bakelite, brass calendar, adjusts from 1948 to 1951, Chevrolet dealer, salesman's name embossed on back, $25

Metal frame, Packard script, 1948, $15

Dinnerware

Demitasse cup, green Overland script/white stoneware, $45

Dinnerplate, 9″, Ford script in dark green, shows Rotunda, Shenango china, $40

Syracuse china, small vegetable dish, decorated with multicolored globe with word "Oldsmobile" above it, $35

Driver's License Holder, leather strap wraps around steering column, California Oldsmobile dealer, late 1940s, $10

Employee Plant Badge

AMC factory, with employee number and window for photo, $25

Autocar plant, oval badge, $50

Cadillac Motor Car Division, hexagon shape, Cadillac logo, shield with wreath, nickle plate, $85

Swirled plastic "perpetual calendar," brass front, 1940s, $40.

Pontiac, child's headdress, late 1950s, Oregon dealer, $35.

Keyfob, Buick, golden anniversary, 1953, $15.

Chrysler plant badge, New Castle, Indiana, metal, $40

Ford Northville Plant, $65

Rogue Plant, Ford Motor Company, $20

Fan, cardboard, shows couple at picnic on front, Ford dealer advertising on back, wooden handle, $10

Film

Fun on Wheels, 16 mm, introduces 1954 Corvette, $250

Plymouth new model announcement with press kit, 1968, $125

Firewall Plate, Auburn logo, with serial number and model number, $75

Flashlight, red plastic, hand-held size, reads "Mopar Parts," 1950s logo, $10

Flyswatter, Chevrolet dealer, wire swatter with a wooden handle, 1940s, $15

Football, small size vinyl, Mayfield Wildcats/Qua Buick, has Wildcat's game schedule, 1970s, $5

Glasses, set of six, clear Fostoria glass, 1" Thunderbird etched in each glass, late 1950s, gift to Fomoco employee, $60 set

Hiphugger Bell-bottom pants, white duck, red and blue "AMC," never worn, $50

Hurricane Lamp, frosted glass, blue letters, "Ford Glass Plant," 1950, $20

Ice Scraper, Pontiac Wide-Track for 1963, red plastic, $5

Indian Headdress, Child's, vinyl headband with multicolored feathers, circa 1953, Oregon dealer, $35

Key Case, leather key holder, advertising for Oklahoma Studebaker dealer, $15

Key Chain, celluloid ID tag, space for name and address, Buick script, 1930s era, Rhode Island dealer, $25

Key Holder, metal, reads "One of the first ten thousand 1939 Buicks," $45

Lamp Bulb Kit, tin, dark blue, white letters read "Genuine Chevrolet Parts," 1930s logo, has most contents, $35

Lapel Pin

Buick 8 in script, "1937 Buick 8, a leader in service progress," enamel with screw back, $55

Buick Hawk, 1980s, $5

Willys Overland Football Club, red/white/blue enamel, screw back, $50

Letter Opener, Oldsmobile, 1950s, $25

License Plate Attachment, Chrysler/Plymouth dealer, Texas, unused, $15

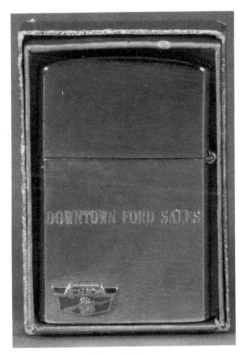

Ford, lighter, 1950s logo, $25.

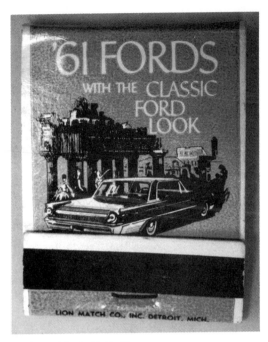

Ford matchbook, 1961, $5.

Light, dealer window decoration, black glass with 1950s-style "Pontiac" script, $50

Lighter
Chief Pontiac logo both sides, 1950s pocket style, $35
Zippo, large desk size, Chrysler logo, $5
Zippo, windproof pocket size, 1950s, Cadillac crest, $40

Lucky Penny, 1955 penny encased in aluminum horseshoe, "Keep me for Good Luck" one side, Chevrolet dealer on reverse, $15

Lunch Cooler, red vinyl, white letters read "Pinto/Coca Cola, the California Compacts," unusual Coca Cola/Pinto collectible, $15

Magnet, vinyl refrigerator magnet, replica of Mustang horse emblem, $5

Matchbook
Fords pictured, 1966, $3
Packard convertible on both sides, 1948, dealer giveaway, $5
Plymouth, 1956, $4

Mechanical Pencil
Chrysler winged wreath logo, souvenir of visit to the Chrysler factory, Detroit, $35

Tiny 1949 Oldsmobile floating in oily substance, $50

Medallion
Brass, 1939, "Be Modern, Buy Chrysler," $20
Heavy bronze color token, 2″ diameter, GM 75th Anniversary, Lansing, Michigan, Oldsmobile logo, $20

Mirror, pocket size, Studebaker Vehicle Works, South Bend, Indiana, $25

Nametag, pinback with attached ribbon, reads "Dodge," souvenir of Chrysler Dealer Preview, New York World's Fair, May 1940, $30

Paper Cups and Plates, 1960s Chevrolet dealer giveaway, bow tie logo, lists models available, including Corvette, $5 set

Paperweight, brass color pot metal figural of the 1902 Nash, 50th Anniversary of the Nash, a nice dealer display item, 1902–52, $95

Pedal Car, 1965 Mustang, by AMF, sold at Christmastime by the Ford dealers, red, excellent white decals, showroom condition, $650

Pen
Fountain, sales award pen and pencil set, $75

Pontiac, mechanical pencil, end shaped like gearshift knob, late 1930s, $35.

Mechanical pencils with oil-filled tops were popular advertising pieces in the 1950s. This one contains a miniature 1954 Oldsmobile, $45.

Nash, fiftieth anniversary paperweight, 1952, $95.

Chevy Time, 1964, *Prophecy* perfume by Prince Matchabelli, $40.

Wooden, advertising for Kissel cars, needs new nib, $20

Pen and Pencil Set, cross, gold "Buick" script, $40 pair

Pencil

Mechanical, 1954 Oldsmobile floating in oil-filled top, this pencil was depicted in Olds sales literature that year, $45

Wooden, 1950s Oldsmobile logo, Jack Frost Motors, Kansas, unsharpened, $3

Pencil Box, copper, 1955 Plymouth salesman's merit award, $35

Perfume, Prince Matchabelli's *Prophecy*, Chevy Time 1964, $40

Pin

"Chrysler Corporation, Official sponsor 1992" with Olympic rings logo, cloisonné, $5

"GM Engineering Staff," diamond chips, $80

"GM/Expo '86," cloisonné, red and blue, $10

Packard Master Serviceman/Partsman, gold, blue, and red cloisonné, $35

Pinback Button

Buick, 1960s, shows fingers making peace sign, with "6" (V6), $5

"Switch to the big 1938 American Beauty— Dodge," 3½" salesman's name at bottom, $25

Tin, reads "New Chevrolet Six, Queen of the Shows," $15

Pin, Chrysler Master Technician Conference, 1930s, $15.

Pin, Corvette Owner, given to Corvette buyers with owner's manual, 1950s, $150.

Pin, Pontiac Service Craftsman, 1930s mechanic's award, $40.

Pin, Mopar Parts & Accessories, $20.

Pin, Packard Wings Award, "Work to Win," WWII era, $45.

Ford, pinback button, 1970s advertising campaign, $5.

Hat pin, Ford NFL punt, pass, kick contestant, $5.

Plaque, Willys-Knight script logo, bronze plaque, 9½″ by 4¾″, "I am the Willys-Knight Engine," describes features, $60

Plate, 1½″ by 2″ metal plate, room to write oil change dates, Pierce Arrow, $25

Playing Cards,
Chevrolet, 1962 model years, shows all models from last fifty years, $50
Jeep Golden Eagle, $15

Pocket Calendar, 1939, Pennsylvania Ford dealer, $10

Pocket Mirror, Pennsylvania Plymouth dealer's name and phone number on back, probably 1930s, $20

Pocketknife, gold, "Cadillac Fifty Years of Craftsmen League, 1935–85," $35

Pot Holder, apple shape, Dodge dealer, 1961, $10

Press Release, introducing 1967 Pontiacs, lots of factory photos, including GTO, $150

Promotional Model Car, Studebaker Commander, cardboard garage box, $400

Sparkalong Burgess battery puzzle, 1952, $25.

Promotional Model Car Display, huge "crystal ball," reads "There's a Ford in your Future," shows seven different promotional models of 1950 models available, $2,500 with correct promos

Puzzle, Chevrolet, world's finest six-cylinder schoolbus, die cut, thirty-five pieces, reversible, 8″ by 14″, boxed, 1932, $60

Record, Ford choir album, Ford logo on label, 1966, $5

Ring, ten karat, ruby chip, Chrysler Corporation logo, $275

Ruler, 15″ wooden ruler, 1938 Pontiac advertising, $30

Sales Award, white ceramic mug showing a 1947 Stakebed truck, gold emblem on bottom reads "1961 Sales Award," one of a set of six, $15 each

Salt and Pepper, red plastic, "Season's Greetings from your Dodge and Plymouth dealer," $5

Screwdriver
Embossed Scripps-Booth Motorcars, $40
Green/white plastic handle reads "Nash," $20

Service Mats, paper mats mechanics used to keep carpet clean, 1964 Chevrolet, $10

Service Pin
Bust of Henry Ford, twenty-five years, ten karat gold, $45
Mechanic's, Cadillac certified craftsman, 1959, screw back enameled lapel pin, crown and shield logo over "V," $60

Service Reminder, tab that hangs from mirror or visor, marmon, space to write mileage of oil change, $60

Chevrolet playing cards, 1965, $15.

Sign

   Brown tin sign, 4″ by 30″, yellow letters read "General Motors," one sided, $90

   Desk size, 6″ by 9″, black metal with red and white letters reads "Dollar for dollar you can't beat Pontiac service," fits in wooden base to sit on service counter, $45

   Figural Indian head, works like a weather vane, Pontiac, $750

   Neon, "Corvair by Chevrolet," 11″ by 4″, gold and white, early 1960s, $350

   Neon, "Desoto Fluid Drive," neon window sign with original transformer, works, $600

   Porcelain, double sided, Willys-Jeep Service, $640

   Porcelain, Oakland-Pontiac, $750

Silverware, fork, Cadillac crest, silver plate, probably from the executive dining room, $35

Statue, chalk ware, "Dodge Safety Sheriff," embossed on base, 16″ tall, cowboy hat, sunglasses, 1970s, $125

Sticker, reflective foil, Ohio Chevrolet dealer, 1960s, $2

Stickpin, Velie, ten karat gold, $45

Sunglasses, 1962 Chevrolet, $10

Tape, cassette, in vinyl folder with sales brochures, 1988 Buick dealer handout, $20 all

Tape, VCR, 1990 Chevrolet Lumina Sneak Preview, $5

Tape Measure

   Blue and yellow Packard script, reads "Ask the man who owns one," $75

   Celluloid, Buick script logo, patent date 1917, $75

Thermometer

   Small desk size on cardboard printed with 1947 calendar, Ford dealer giveaway, $25

Chevrolet, Flint Plant, tape measure, $20.

Tie bar, winged Mercury, $25.

Willys Cars, Trucks, Jeeps porcelain sign with neon, two transformers, $1,200.

Reflective sticker, Ohio dealer, $2.

Tin wall model, 1970s reproduction, shows some wear, "Packard Authorized Service," $15

Thimble, plastic, Indiana Chevrolet dealer giveaway, 1960s, $5

Tie bar and cuff link set, 1950s Cadillac emblem, sterling, $60

Tin

Buick-approved accessory, Cooling System Rust Inhibitor, light blue tin, red letters, $25

Delco Shock fluid (hydraulic) dated 1938, $35

Ford Fabric Protector, sixteen ounces, dated 1966, $12

GM Blue Coral, 1950s-era Pontiac logo, $25

Mopar Power Steering Fluid, quart, $20

Tire Pressure Gauge

Ford Crest on dial, 1950s, $50

Peerless gold eagle with wings outspread logo, stick type, $50

Token, brass, "Free Winter Inspection," Chevrolet bow tie logo, $5

Tool, open-end wrench, Maxwell script, $15

Tool Check

Autocar Company, brass, $5

Marmon, letter "M" in wreath logo, $25

Oldsmobile, zinc, $10

Royal Motor Car Company, Cleveland, $20

Tin, Pontiac Blue Coral wax, $25.

Tray, tin serving tray, 1957 Pontiac advertising, $50

Uniform, old Ford logo, mechanic's overalls, vg, 1950s, $25

Watch Fob

Chevrolet, 1939, one of the minor prizes given away on the Sophie Tucker radio show, first prize was a new Chevy, fob value, $60

Hupmobile, $125

Tin, Buick Cooling System Rust Inhibitor, $25.

Tin, GM Rear Axle Lubricant, $15.

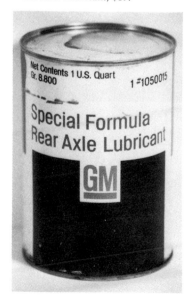

Delco one gallon hydraulic brake fluid tin, $25.

Tin, Mopar Glass Cleaner, 1960s, $10.

Folding yardstick, 1963, Ford, $20.

Watchband Calendar, small tin monthly calendars
    given to truck salesmen, tabs fold over
    watchband, $5

Yardstick
    Chevrolets, 1962, "A New World of Worth,"
        $15

Cube shape, used to check level of gas tank,
    1908 Ford advertising, $50

Yo-Yo, wooden, advertising 1955 Chevrolet, $15

2

Customizing Items and Accessories

The first thing anyone does with a new car is to customize it. Whether you add an expensive new stereo, sheepskin seat covers, or just a bumper sticker, personalization of your car makes a statement about you.

Accessorization probably began with the purchase of the first automobile. Americans have never been able to leave a motorcar alone; they always manage to think of a few necessities to add that the factory failed to install.

At first, early motorists added little homey touches, such as buffalo lap robes and flower vases. Personalization accelerated with the coming of Henry Ford's Model T. This utilitarian vehicle was affordable but plain. Even the Ford dealers had a standing joke that the Model T was available in any color so long as it was black. Motorists imaginatively thought of ways to make their T stand out in a crowd. It is estimated that over the nineteen years that the Model T was built, more than fifty thousand accessories for it were developed by enterprising businessmen and by the Model T owners themselves.

Companies began to offer a wide array of automobile accessories to motorists. At the 1916 Auto Show, many new accessories designed especially for women drivers and passengers were introduced. A colorful pinstripe here, a leather-covered trunk for traveling, a woven wool lap robe, a pair of matching carnival glass bud vases, a figural radiator mascot shaped like a demon thumbing his nose at the world all found their way onto many early vehicles. Many auto interiors included vanity cases, mirrors, and even smelling salts. Some accessories, such as turn signals, horns, and windshield defrosters, made the automobile safer to drive. Others involved creature comforts, such as cigarette lighters, radios, clocks, and fancy swirled glass gearshift knobs. Other aftermarket products offered for the public's enjoyment were flag holders that attached to radiator caps, motometers to monitor the engine temperature, and beautifully designed radiator ornaments. These mascots are often considered works of art in their own right, especially the crystal ornaments designed by Rene Lalique.

Casco was one of the premier makers of cigarette lighters. At first, they made add-on lighters and swing-out ashtrays. Lighters were sold for $1.75. A swing-out ashcup and the lighter were available in combination for $3. These are collected for their chrome parts and colorful Bakelite knobs. By the 1930s, Casco was manufacturing 98 percent of the smoking accessories installed by American automakers.

Rearview mirrors and turn signals were also popular additions to the 1930s automobiles. The Turn Signal Corporation cleverly advertised their product with the slogan, "The man behind can't read your mind."

Leather-trimmed and metal trunks were popular throughout the 1910s and 1920s. This accessory all but disappeared in the 1930s, when automakers built a trunk into their sedans.

About the same time, radios became one of the most desirable auto accessories. More than 500,000 sets were installed in new and used cars in 1933 alone. Crosley advertised its Roamio unit for $75 plus installation. Record players were also available. In the 1950s, many automakers offered radios and phonographs that slid out from under the dash to be used at picnics or at the beach. These portable, battery-powered units are very collectible today. They are difficult to find as many of them were pulled out and lost or damaged.

That first teardrop-shaped camp trailer carried provisions and even offered clean and dry—although somewhat cramped—sleeping accommodations. These graceful little trailers are being reproduced today and still look great behind that vintage automobile.

As the automobile industry grew, so did the market for unique, one-of-a-kind transportation. In the 1920s and 1930s, many custom

coach builders took mass-produced automobiles and turned them into luxurious customized vehicles for American movie stars and for royalty around the world. The installation of mink or fox upholstery, beautiful woodwork, as well as special body panels and sometimes even gold-plated trim, made these early limousines remarkable.

By the 1940s, the demands of war had affected the world's economy. Orders for specialty vehicles were almost nil, and custom-body builders turned their considerable talents to building ambulances and military staff cars. The early custom-bodied vehicles had stirred the imagination of the common man. The whole idea of accessorization seemed to escalate, peaking in the Fab Fifties. Before World War II, kids were likely to take the fenders off dad's old Ford and drop in a larger motor, but modifications in the 1950s and 1960s soared beyond the imagination of the 1930s and 1940s teens. The 1950s would be remembered as *the* decade of customization. Mile-long continental kits, bulging bubble fender skirts, chromed lake pipes, leather tuck-and-roll upholstery, and humongous spinner hubcaps were the norm. Talk about wretched excess, we just didn't know when to quit. It was in this era of frenched taillights and chopped and channeled deuces that such master craftsmen as Ed ("Big Daddy") Roth and George Barris created some of the most outrageously customized automobiles ever.

Automakers had always produced "dream cars" for the auto shows—elaborately customized, futuristic automobiles. Soon talented hobbyists were building their own super-customs in their backyards. Some of the more creative minds—such as Daryl Starbird, Ed Roth, and Boyd Coddington—were soon asked to help out their friends on projects. This, quite naturally, led into the business of customizing. The growth of the outrageous California car culture was fueled by publicity sparked by these supercustom hot rods being built there. They were, quite naturally, publi-

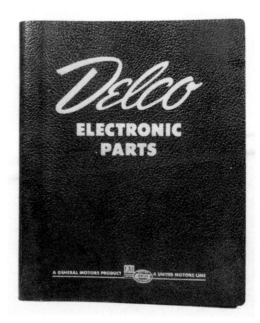

Knock-offs, add-on spinners for custom wheels, NOS, $50.

Notebook, Delco Electronic Parts, GM, $5.

cized in the national car magazines, many of which were based in California. This was the beginning of a nationwide customizing binge that probably peaked in the 1960s with the Batmobile.

The desire to have a car that is different from all others has contributed to the multi-million-dollar business of selling automotive accessories. From the early Sears and Roebuck catalogs, mid-1950s catalogs from Honest Charley's Speed Shop, and current offerings from J. C. Whitney, mail-order car parts and accessories sold well. Older catalogs themselves are popular with collectors today, and they are fun to look through. Imagine buying a vacuum-operated Hollywood wolf whistle for only $2.95!

One of the most popular chain stores was the Pep Boys. Advertising figures, matchbooks, oilcans, lighter fluid tins, and tire patch kits with the cigar-smoking Manny, Moe, and Jack are all sought after today. One of the most popular Pep Boys collectibles is

the Western oilcan. A typical Western desert scene with Manny, Moe, and Jack trying to stay astride a bucking bronco decorates the front of the can.

Few old-car enthusiasts do not recognize the yellow "Moon" eyes decal, a staple for yesteryear's racing fans. Today, the same person who added that "Moon" decal in the 1960s is likely to be scraping it off. He also probably threw away the hubcaps and plain rims from his 1966 Mustang as soon as he could afford mag wheels and today is spending a lot of time haunting flea markets and auto swaps hunting for four original hubcaps for his restoration project.

Today, few of these custom cars still exist, and the ones that do are usually very well preserved and shown regularly. In the 1970s, much of this creativity was turned loose on vans; many of today's elaborate van conversions got their start through the efforts of young customizers in the 1970s to turn out a van with every possible option. There are efforts today, by young people and older folks alike, to customize even their new cars. Witness the proliferation of lowered minitrucks with enormous stereo systems. It's the American dream—buy a new car and then customize it!

Accelerator Footrest, rubber pad bolts to floorboards, Stanwood Company, NOS with original box, $20

Antitheft Device

Auto Theft Signal System, keys, patent date 1914, $90

Defender thief-proof lock, key lock fits over coil box switch, $45

Ashtray

Dark blue and cream glass swirl, add-on ashtray, hangs under dash, $45

Metal Snap-On Tools, 5″ by 7″, $10

Metal, Victor Gaskets, 4″ diameter, $20

Bank

Big A Auto Parts, 1918 Runabout replica, Ertl, 1991 edition, No. 5 in series, about ⅕ scale, $25

Eastwood Company, 1950 Chevrolet panel truck, Ertl, about ⅕ scale, dated 1989 on

Pre-1950s battery charger, 6 volt, $65.

rear doors, No. 1 in series, very low production, $425

Tin, battery shaped, Atlas battery advertising premium, $50

Bendy, flexible vinyl figure, "Champ Man," Champion Spark Plugs advertising figure, copyright date 1990, $10

Bobbing Head Dog, eyes light up when brake pedal is depressed, $50

Brass Carriage-Type Lamp, kerosene, $75

Bud Vase(s)

Matched pair with brackets, Tree of Life pattern, $200 pair

Vaseline glass, Finecut and Daisy pattern with original metal bracket, $45

Carhop Tray, mounts on car window, 1950s, $25

Catalog

J. C. Whitney, 1959, lots of accessories and parts, $20

Pep Boys, 1958, full line of auto accessories, bicycles, wagons, and toys, $25

"Sure Fit Fabrics," 1927, tops, seat covers, catalog contains many fabric samples of the era, such as mohair, $50

Western Auto Stores, 1927 Ford Owners Supply Book, includes seat covers to parts, 128 pages, $35

Cigarette Lighter, Casco, opalescent "Onyxoid" knob glows when lighter is hot, NOS, $25

Clock

Neon, "Napa Auto Parts," blue/yellow logo, 1970s, $45

Rearview mirror, New Haven stem-wind, thirty-hour clock, radium hands, NOS in original box, $200

Continental Kit, extended bumper, l-o-o-o-ng, Hallcraft add-on for 1958 Cadillac, used, very good, $1,200

Cup, pewter, "Acme Automotive Finishes," $20

Curb Feelers

Clamp to fender wells, chrome, mint and boxed, $15

Electric buzzer sounds when feeler touches

Pontiac accessory continental kit, 1958, $450.

Door guards, early 1960s, NOS, $15.

Dur-A-cloth artificial chamois, $15.

curb, mint sent in original box with instructions, $50

Decal
   B&M Hydrostick, shows robot shifting gears, $10
   Clay Smith Cams, mean-looking woodpecker, cigar clamped in teeth, "Mr. Horsepower," $10
   Yellow with large eyes, "Moon Equipped," $10

Deflector, yellow plastic window deflectors fit in front of vent window on most older cars, NOS set, $50

Defroster, suction cups mount electric defroster to windshield, 1930s accessory, NOS, with original box and instructions, $60

Display Rack, black and yellow metal, B-K radiator caps and gas tank caps, 1950s, $35

Door Guards, cream-colored, hard plastic, clamp to edge of door to preven dents, mint on card, $15

Drive-In Speakers, good condition with wiring, $30

Dur-a-cloth, probably the first artificial chamois, mint, unused cloth with colorful cardboard box featuring generic 1940s-era auto, $15

Duster, lady's linen coat to protect clothing while driving, off-white, $50

Employee Badge, Motor Wheel Corporation, $40

Exhaust Whistle, Liberty siren, NOS, $175

Fender Skirts
   Cruiser skirts, NOS, steel with stainless trim, scuff plates and all hardware, $350
   Fiberglass, fits 1957 Chevy, $100

Fire Extinguisher, brass with mounting bracket, Pyrene, $50

Fire extinguisher with mounting bracket, $10.

First-Aid Kit, Johnson and Johnson First-Aid Autokit, 5″ by 7½″ tin with contents, how-to booklet dated 1942, $25

Flag Holder, straps around radiator cap, gold color shield with red and blue enamel, patent date 1927, holds five original flags, $75

Fog Lights, chrome with amber lenses, attached to front bumper, well used, few pits in chrome, $50 pair

Fuzzy Dice

Large, 4″ diameter, white with black dots, $5

White silk, 3″ square, red and blue bicentennial scenes, $5

Flag holder, mounts to radiator cap, 1927, $75.

Gasoline Gauge, Atwater Kent, patent 1909, $35

Gearshift Knob

Glass swirl, navy blue, cream swirls, 2″ diameter, $50

Green dice, orange dots, gaudy plastic, $35

Red plastic, tapered sides, red jewel in center, $25

Simulated onyx, brass Saint Christopher medal in center, $25

Glare Shield, Emko, green plastic strip affixes to windshield, in original paper envelope showing 1940s auto dashboard, $10

Glasses, set of six, painted like the familiar blue STP cans, probably 1960s, $12 set

Gloves, black leather, long gauntlet-style gloves, $35

Goggles, glass lenses, oilcloth, ties on behind head, $75

Grill Attachment, cloisonné, shows 1950s race car, souvenir of Florida, clamps to grill supports, $25

Hat, ladies large bonnet, veil, ties to hold hat in place while motoring, $45

Helmet, brown leather racing helmet, some aging, $75

Hood Ornament, steer horns (Texas longhorn), just right for the cowboy Cadillac, $50

Horn, bulb type, $75

Emko Glare Shields, NOS, original envelope, $10.

Leather goggles, tinted lenses, $40.

Grill attachment, "USA," $12.

Horn Button

Add on, Sparton multitone, straps to steering column, $35

APCO accessory bolts to steering column, NOS, $20

Hubcap(s)

"Baby moons," small, smooth chrome hubcaps, set of four, $40

Spinner hubcaps, a 1950s rage, $20–$30 each.

"Flipper," chrome darlings of 1950s hot-rodders, fancy chrome hubcaps with three-pronged spinners, set of four, 15″ tires, $90

"Full moons," full-size smooth wheel covers, set of four, for 15″ tires, $75

Pasco screw-on hubcap, approximately 4″ diameter, nickle-plated brass, few scuff marks, $50

Lamp

Brass lamp, acetylene gas, round, 8″ diameter, $75

Kerosene, square carriage style, $60

Lap Robe

Buffalo skin, $250

Wool, $75

Lapel Pin, Snap on Tools, screwdriver shape, 1980s, $10

Letter Opener

Cincinnati Vector Auto Lamp Company, 12″ long, silver, engraved handle, $35

Keystone Spring Works, embossed brass letter opener, 50th Anniversary, 1870–1920, $35

Lighter, Hester battery logo, Zippo-type lighter, $20

Lint Brush, ceramic top is figural 1950s Corvette, 1980s, $5

Medallion, brass, Prudential Insurance 50th Anniversary, 1875–1925, has the "rock" logo, presentation box, $40

Mirror(s)

Rearview, Argus, about 1910, $45

Vanity Visor Mirror, aftermarket, has place to pencil-in service and travel record, $15

Vanity Visor Mirror, in elaborate Bakelite frame, with cutout birds and flowers, $20

Yankee sideview mirrors, mint in colorful original box, clamp to front door post, chrome, $45

Money Clip, Prestone antifreeze, $10

Motometer

Boyce, dog bone radiator cap, 8″ tall, $75

Boyce, working condition, 3½″ diameter, $50

Nameplate, Hayes Body Corporation, brass, $40

Nodder, for back window, nodding plush puppy, eyes light up when brakes are applied, made in Japan, $45

Paperweight, C&D Battery, figural car battery, $35

Parking Meter, double head on a single post, working order with keys, $50

Water temperature gauge, aftermarket item, 1961 Chevrolet on box, $25.

Universal Batteries, playing cards, two decks, $20.

Dog nodder, Japan, $45.

Pinback Button
  AC Spark Plugs, shows their mascot horse, "Sparky," 1950s era, $5
  Delco Save-a-Battery program, World War II era, $15
Playing Cards, Universal batteries, double deck,

one blue, one maroon with gold letters "Universal" in 1930s heart logo, $20
Pocket Protector, vinyl, McCord Performance gaskets, $2
Poodle Skirt, gray felt, pink poodle, 1950s, excellent, $30
Raccoon Tail, great antenna decoration, good condition, $15
Radiator Mascot
  Chromed diving nude, with bracket, copyright date 1920, very graceful, $250
  Essex, 1928 goddess, $225
  Ford, 1936 accessory greyhound, $200
  Frosted glass, woman's face with long, flowing hair, Corning Glass Works, $300
  Price Auto Service advertising, nickle-plated brass, Kansas dealer, $135
Radio, Crosley Roamio, "the amazing automobile receiving set," price in 1932 was $75 plus installation, today only $250
Reflector
  More than thirty red jewels, 5" diameter, Do-Ray Safety Signal, $20
  Red lens, arm swings down in back window to warn other motorists, $20
  Tin litho base, red plastic reflector, stands in rear window to warn oncoming motorists, 1950s, $15
Ruler
  Creston Auto Supply (Iowa), 1960, 36" metal ruler rolls up for storage, $10
  Crosley radios, triangle shape, $12

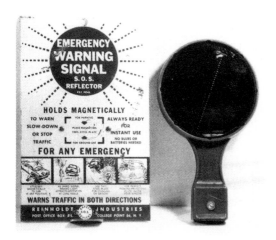

Back window safety reflector, 1950s, $15.

Green plastic steering wheel knob, $25.

Service Pin

Harrison Radiator service pin, twenty-five years, hexagon, $15

Worthington Engines, 10KGF, $20

Sign

Porcelain, Polarine Oil and Greases for Motors, blue and white, $150

Tin, AC Speedometer for Fords, shows speedometer and spoked wheels, $450

Tin, Champion Spark Plugs, 1960s, $60

Tin, Powell Mufflers, shows 1930s car, warns of dangers of carbon monoxide, $250

Tin, Weed Tire Chains, enameled, shows white tire on spoke rim, dial turns to show price of gas, goes up to thirty nine cents a gallon, $150

Spare Tire Lock, NOS with key, heavy cable slips around spare and hanger, 1920s and 1930s vintage, $40

Spark Plug

Blue-topped porcelain, $15

Champion priming cup, $35

Champion Y-4-A, for 1930s Chevrolets, mint, unused in old-style blue and white box with globe logo, $5

Motormaster Blue Crown, $5

Spitfire, Lightning Bolt logo, $10

Splitdorf, brass plug, mica core, $20

Spark Plug Gap Tool, marked "AC Spark Plugs," $5

Spotlights, dummy spotlights (nonoperating), with mirrors on back, swirled plastic handles, $100 pair

Steering Wheel Knob

Ivory glass, yellow and blue swirls, "Rotary International" in center, $45

White plastic, clear insert reads "Rod and Custom" logo in center (old *Street Rod* magazine), $25

Stop Indicator

Mounts in rear window, policeman figure, arms swing out when brake pedal is depressed, $75

Mounts in rear window, traffic light with red, yellow, and green lenses that light up when brakes are applied, $60

Sunshade, cobalt blue, elaborate heavy mechanism holds it in place above windshield, swings down for use, 1930s era, $50

Sunvisor, add-on accessory, metal with chrome trim, stationary, $175

Switch, Ark-les Fog Light Switch, NOS, $15

Taillight Lens, marked "Stop/Safety First," red glass, $15

Tape Measure, Stromberg vis-a-gas carburetor, celluloid advertising tape measure, $35

Tie Bar, AC Spark Plug, Advisory Council, 1961, red cloisonné map of the United States, $15

Tie Clasp, A-C Delco, figural spark plug, 1990s, $10

Bull Dog Friction Tape tin, $12.

Delco-Light Oil tin, $20.

Atlas Door-Ease stick, tin, $5.

Varsity Vinyl Top Dressing Tin, Pep Boys, $25.

Hastings compression tester, mint with contents, $40.

Tie Tack, Motor Trend Car of the Year, Pontiac Grand Prix, $5

Tin

Acme Glass Fuses, orange/blue tin with contents, $5

Atlas polishing cloth, mint, red/blue tin, cloth unused, $15

Cross Country (Sears before Allstate), shock absorber fluid, blue and orange tin, U.S. map outline, light scratches, $25

Atlas polishing cloth tin, mint, $15.

Universal Top Oiler, 1930s, aftermarket item, $25.

Bowes Seal Fast fuse tin, $6.

Swing-Out Tissue Dispenser, 1950s, MIB, $50.

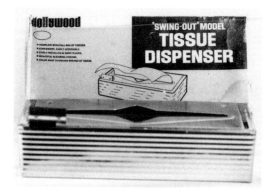

Pep Boys, Varsity Vinyl Top Dressing, 1960s, unused with original price sticker, $25

Phillips Automobile Screws, Assortment No. 31, black square tin with compartments, contains trim and upholstery screws, 1930s, $25

Western Auto Polishing Cloth, mint, tin with cloth, $10

Tissue Dispenser, Hollywood brand, swing-out dispenser fits under dash, NOS, original box, $50

Top Oiler

Accessory oiler (before oil filters), Whiz, $40

White milk glass oiler, with low oil indicator light, NOS, $95

Trunk, Kari-Keen luggage carrier, clamps to rear of car, swings open to hold suitcases, steel, chrome trim, good original paint, $150, repainted, $95

Turn Signal, add-on accessory kit clamps to steering column, $45

Watch Fob, *American Automobile Digest*, winged wheel logo, gold in color, $35

Windshield Defroster, Casco electric sleet remover, suction cups attach to windshield, heating element in glass, NOS, $45

3

Auto Club Memorabilia

Automobile clubs started out as social organizations, little more than a group of friends enjoying an afternoon drive in the country, picnicking, and lending a helping hand with any needed repairs. Besides, fending off the insults of the nonmotoring public was easier when automobiles outnumbered wagons. In those days, it was helpful to take someone along who knew the way. No road signs existed and unmarked roads were navigated by using familiar landmarks or advertising signs for country stores and inns.

These pleasant outings convinced the automobile owners that they must act cooperatively. Their first venture into mutual aid was the posting of road signs at local intersections so that motorists could enjoy clearly marked routes from one city to another. One of the first posted interstate routes in the United States was the road from New York City to Boston. Signs for this trip were prepared and erected by the large and active automobile clubs in New York City and Boston with the cooperation of the smaller clubs at points in between. Early automobile club road signs did not just give speed limits or point out directions. They showed the mileage between two points and warned of local hazards, such as deep mud or the constable's speed trap.

It is difficult for modern auto hobbyists to realize just how much opposition greeted the early motorists. The "get a horse" crowd did all they could to discourage what they called the dangerous sport of motoring. Automobile owners were subjected to restrictive legislation, hazardous roads, and the disdain of much of the population. As the number of motorcars on the road increased, many unfair and unreasonable restrictions on motorcar operators were passed. One town went so far as to propose a law that prohibited the storage of gasoline in moving vehicles. This law, of course, would have made it impossible to drive a motorcar in that town. It's no wonder that automobile enthusiasts decided to band

National Automobile Club Touring Guide, $12.

together for their common good and safety.

The American Motor League founded in Chicago in 1895 is usually recognized as the first car club in the United States. Other regional clubs soon followed, such as the Philadelphia Automobile Club, the Automobile Club of America (ACA), and the Rhode Island Automobile Club.

These clubs and many other regional groups were active in local politics. Early car club members felt that were not accomplishing their goals as quickly as they had hoped. By 1902, frustrated with the lack of local and federal government attention to their needs, they joined forces to form the American Automobile Association (AAA). Thirty-six local clubs supported the national organization, with each affiliated club al-

lowed a say in the operation of the AAA. At that time, all thirty-six member clubs hailed from the northeast, with nine from New York State alone.

The AAA was instrumental in lobbying for good roads and well-marked routes. In fact, a donation of $10,000 from one of the local clubs was used to support lobbying efforts that promoted the passage of the Brownlow-Latimer Good Roads Bill, the first legislation of its kind in Congress. Almost one hundred years later, the AAA is still serving the needs of the motorist.

Today, people who love old cars still get together. It has been said that if a manufacturer made more than one of any kind of car, those two owners would find one another and form a club. Most current clubs are owners' groups, although a sincere interest in the marque, not ownership, is usually the only requirement for membership.

The first antique automobile collector's club in the United States was the Antique Automobile Club of America (AACA), formed in 1935 by fourteen members. Their first annual meeting was in Philadelphia in March 1936. Regional chapters quickly followed. Their first annual meeting was held in 1936 at the Devon Horse Show grounds near Philadelphia, but the AACA annual fall show quickly outgrew this facility. In 1954, the AACA moved this popular show and its fast-growing flea market to Hershey, where it has flourished. Today, AACA is more than fifty thousand members strong and Hershey is the car lover's mecca. Thousands of vendors attend from all over the United States to buy, sell, trade, and swap stories with the auto hobbyists from all over the world who journey to Hershey each fall.

The mid-1930s was a historic time for the founding of car clubs in this country. Interest in preserving the premier American automobiles and the memories of the men who created them was high. About this time, auto enthusiasts in the West were getting together. In 1937, the Horseless Carriage Club of America was organized as the result of a friendly discussion among a small group of California car owners. The club they founded has since grown to more than ten thousand members nationwide. At about the same time, a group of New England old-car lovers formed the Veteran Motor Car Club of America (VMCCA). One of the first organized VMCCA events was a 1940 Easter parade of historic vehicles in New York City. Their membership today numbers more than six thousand.

Although car club activities were pretty much curtailed by World War II, the 1950s were a different story. Automobiles had become an indispensable part of American life, and interest in old cars and hot rods was high. Hundreds of clubs that were founded in that era are still active today. Almost every automobile ever manufactured has at one time or another had its own club. The Studebaker Driver's Club, Vintage Chevrolet Club, Packard Club, Jordan Register, Auburn-Cord-Duesenberg Club, and the Ranchero Club are just a few examples.

One of the most popular clubs west of the Mississippi was formed in 1957. A group of street rod enthusiasts organized with a mission to preserve what they called the traditional California-style hot rod roadster. The Los Angeles Roadsters annual Roadster Exhibition and Swap Meet has become a tradition. Roadster lovers from all over the West cruise to Los Angeles to participate in the Father's Day show.

Today, modern car clubs often act as a clearinghouse for available parts and for restoration information. Many national clubs maintain a reference library of books and literature pertaining to their marque. Some clubs even maintain their own museum, such as the VMCCA's Museum of Transportation in Massachusetts.

Most national clubs publish a newsletter every month or two while their affiliated chapters remain free to publish their own newsletters. Local chapters usually publish a modest paper loaded with club gossip, ads for cars and parts, minutes of the last meeting, a treasurer's report, and the time and location of the next meeting. Quite a large collection of club newsletters can be put together with a minimal investment. They will usually contain a lot of technical data, factory part numbers, factory photos, and restoration tips. It is also entertaining to read some of the cars for sale ads from the older newsletters published in the 1950s and 1960s. What deals!

Clubs usually sponsor a national meet, where members from all parts of the country get together to show off their cars and swap parts and stories about the "one that got away." The real stars of these events are not the beautifully restored vintage automobiles but the club members. These tireless volunteers put in countless hours parking show cars, grilling hot dogs, placating angry swap meet vendors, and even collecting trash. Only

Chrysler Products Restorers Club program, 1966 national meet, $10.

after working a few hours at a club event do you truly appreciated the effort behind a smooth-running and well-organized car show.

In the automotive hobby, history has a way of repeating itself. While many of the ACA's first acts were to lobby for better roads, antique car clubs today see a need to be politically aware and active. Many clubs have banded together to create a state council to serve as a political action machine to preserve our right to own and operate vintage cars. A newly formed group is the World Organization of Automotive Hobbyists (WOAH) which plans to address such issues as restrictive zoning ordinances, the introduction of "clunker bills" whose admitted aim is to remove old cars from the roads, and other problems plaguing old-car hobbyists.

Car club membership has never been so high as it is today. The reason many antique car clubs thrive is no different than it was in the early days of motoring. Old-car lovers welcome the opportunity to spend time with others with like interests, to help one another locate obsolete parts, to give assistance with repairs, and, of course, to show off their cars, many times for the benefit of local charities.

Decal, Chrysler Products Restorers Club, $5.

Then, as now, a group of vintage motorcars on tour draws attention. However, instead of hearing calls of "get a horse," club members today hear whistles and get a "thumbs up" sign for driving beautifully maintained, rolling pieces of American history.

Ashtray
    Chicago Motor Club Honor member, heavy gold-colored, cloisonné stand-up emblem in center, $40
    Metal, A-C-D Club logo (Auburn, Cord, Duesenberg), $15

Badge
    AAA Award, dated 1953, $25
    AAA Detroit, membership badge, white porcelain, $30

Cigar Box, wooden, Illinois Automobile Club, $20

Compact, ladies', brass color, applied cloisonné insigna with red star, "Chicago Motor Club Honor Member," Elgin, $35

Dash Plaque
    Buick Club of America, annual meet, shows 1914 Buick with American flags, July 1976, $6

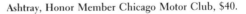

Ashtray, Honor Member Chicago Motor Club, $40.

Chicago Motor Club Honor Member ladies' compact, $35.

Chrysler Products Restorer's Club, third annual meet, June 28–30, Detroit, Michigan, 1965, $8

Classic Chevy Club International, Rocky Mountain Regional Meet, July 1980, Colorado Springs, Colorado, $5

Lincoln Owners Club, third annual meet, 1961, 2½″ by 4″, $8

Desk Ornament, Lucite, 1902–62, 60th Anniversary of the American Automobile Association, $10

Grill Emblem (sometimes called radiator emblem)

AAA National Award, $10

Dash plaque, Pocono Mountain Street Rods, $5.

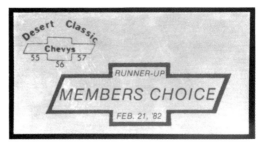

Desert Classic Chevys award, dash plaque, 1982, $3.

Classic Car Club of America, cloisonné, $20

Keystone Automobile Club, cloisonné, blue, gold, and white, $25

Waterloo Iowa Motor Club, enameled emblem, deeply embossed with eagle, radiator, and wheel, 3″ diameter, $40

Key Chain

AAA Golden Wheel Driving Award, $10

Lost key registry, AAA, $3

Key Fob, National Safety Council, nine-year Safe Driver Award, $35

National Safety Council Safe Driver Award key fob, $35.

Lapel Pin

AAA Stop-Look-Listen Club of Michigan, green/white, $5

American Automobile Association, Safety Patrol, school crossing safety program, $15

Bronze pin, 3″, very detailed, engraved with replica of Glidden Trophy, $125

Bugatti Owners club, oval, blue, and gold cloisonné, $15

Children's Day Automobile Club, 1911, photo of child inserted into pin, $20

Gypsy Tour, 1954, gold and red cloisonné pin with safety catch, $25

Mercury Club, screw back, shows the god Mercury, blue cloisonné on silver, $20

UAW/AFL membership, 1945, gold-tone pin with red/white/blue enamel logo showing old car, $20

Willys-Overland Football Club, red/white/blue, screw back, $50

"Worldwide Old Car Club," cloisonné, screw back, shows radiator and headlights of old car, $10

License Plate Attachment

Auburn-Cord-Duesenberg Club, $40

Automobile Legal Association, blue, white, and silver, $15

Cincinnati Automobile Club, oval, $15

"Count on Me to Prevent Accidents," orange/

blue/white, New London Safety Council, 1936, $35

Keystone Automobile Club, cloisonné, blue/gold/white, $25

Rolls Royce Owners Club, cloisonné, 4″ diameter, $20

Map

Baltimore, Maryland, published by Keystone Automobile Club, with headquarters in Philadelphia, late 1920s, $5

Illinois and Indiana, AAA, 1955, $3

Southern California, Automobile Club of Southern California, mission on cover, 1940s, $4

Medallion, 1959 Glidden Tour, 4″ diameter, bronze, blue enameled background, 3″ trophy embossed in center, $100

Membership Cards, roster, flyers, newsletters of the Horseless Carriage Club from 1941–47, collection of twenty-nine different items, $250

Map, Automobile Club of Southern California, 1950s, $3.

UAW-AFL membership pin, 1945, $20.

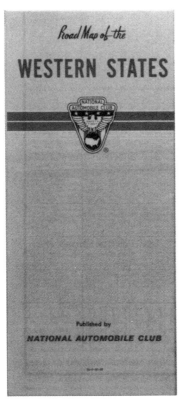

Map, western states, National Automobile Club, $5.

Map, Ocean Highway Association, Florida to New York, $3.

Map, Baltimore, Maryland, Keystone Automobile Club, $5

Mug, pewter, "LA Roadsters," given to participants in the annual Father's Day car show, made in England, $35

Necklace, United Auto Workers (UAW), gold medallion with blue stones, $25

Newsletter

Late Great Chevys, 1958–64 model years included, color cover, March 1981 edition, $3

The Motorcyclist, magazine of the American Motorcycle Association, May 1937, $10

Wing News, newsletter of Chrysler Products Restorers Club, volume 11, numbers 1–12, 1964, $24 all

Paperweight

AAA 60th Anniversary, 1962, bronze, 2½" medallion embedded in Lucite, $20

Heavy bronze, 3" diameter, United Auto Workers, $20

Marble base, red and gold medallion showing

Wing News, Chrysler Products Restorers Club newsletter, June, 1964, $5.

old truck, "Hershey Region, AACA, chartered 1955," with original box, $15

Patch

AAA logo in white on blue field, $2

Embroidered logo of Classic Chevy Club International, 5″ by 7″ large patch, shows 1957 turquoise Chevrolet hardtop, $8

Embroidered winged Chrysler logo, Chrysler Products Restorers Club, 1960s, $10

Pin, Wisconsin Safety League, blue/white, flag logo, 45

United Auto Workers, 1938 monthly membership pins, $3 each.

Pinback Button

AAA Convention in Buffalo, 1908, numbered, has a red, white, and blue attached ribbon, $35

Drivers and Helpers Union, 1908, $25

United Automobile Workers of America, 1″, January 1938, shows 1930s sedan, $5

Plaque

Buick Club of America, 6″ by 8″, 75th Anniversary meet, 1978, silver and black, mounted on wood, MIB, $20

Cast aluminum plaque, popular with street rod clubs of the 1950s, says "Roadsters, Los Angeles — since 1957," with topless street rod, $25

Playing Cards, AAA, 1950s generic-type cars, nice scene, road, hills, and lighthouse, complete double decks, original box, $20

Radiator Badge, cloisonné, Classic Car Club of America, $25

Route Card, Chicago Motor Club, shows route from Erie, Pennsylvania, to Cleveland, Ohio, 1920s, $5

Model A Restorers Club award plaque, $5.

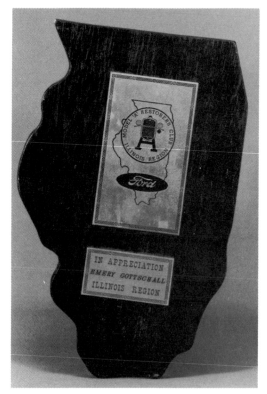

AAA playing cards, 1950s, nice scene, $20.

California State Automobile Association stop sign, $75.

National Corvette Restorers Society necktie, $25.

Chicago Motor Club Route Card, 1930s, $5.

Sign

Porcelain on steel, directional sign, Locust Valley, Glencove, erected by Long Island Automobile Club, $200

Porcelain on steel, directional sign, water, four miles, and Barstow, sixty-eight miles, logo of Auto Club of Southern California, few bullet holes, $125

Tie, dark blue with stripes, decorated with tiny Corvette flags, with "NCRS" underneath logo, National Corvette Restorer's Society, $25

Tie Tack

AMA Tour Award (American Motorcycle Association), 1972, gold with blue enamel, $15

Harley Owners Group, nice detail, $15

Token, Reading Coin Club, shows Duryea, $10

Trophy

Chrysler Products Restorers Club, 1966 Annual Meet, Manheim, Pennsylvania, May 14–15, 1966, "Best DeSoto," $50

Concurs d'Elegance, Southern California annual benefit car show, 1962, best of class, $125

Watch Fob, colorful 1½" diameter, Automobile Club of Southern California, $25

4

Automotive Art

Automotive art is enjoying a great deal of popularity at the moment. This area of the automobile hobby has always had its die-hard fans, but recent works by some talented artists have increased collector interest. The works of modern American automotive artists, such as Ken Dallison, Nancy Graham, Ken Eberts, and Stanley Wanlass, are collected with as much enthusiasm as the older automotive art by Peter Helck, J. C. Leyendecker, and Leslie Saalburg.

Automotive art is not limited to just art collectors but includes thousands of old-car nuts who want any and all kinds of automobile-related art. Postcards, oil paintings, and watercolors, along with photographs, illustrations, posters, magazine covers, advertising, and sculpture representing the motorcar are avidly sought by collectors.

Art is an investment, one that gives the owner great pleasure in displaying it. This combination makes collecting automotive art especially appealing to the old-car enthusiast. Modern artwork is still reasonably priced but older works of art, particularly racing scenes, are selling at the higher end of the scale. Automotive prints, as well as original artwork, are in demand. One of the most popular prints is a series of eight early racing scenes by Peter Helck that appeared in *Esquire*.

Print, limited edition, Ken Dallison, available only through a mail-in offer, $25.

Print, Ken Dallison, Oldsmobile 442, $25.

Early automobile racing captured the imagination of the artists and illustrators of the day. The French artist Edouard Montaut was fond of attending the automobile races around Paris and sketching the day's events. He would then return to his studio, where his assistants would turn out lithographs of his day's work. From 1904 until his death in 1909, his shop produced thousands of early auto racing scenes. Montaut's hand-colored prints were sensitive to sunlight; thus, it is difficult to find one in which the colors have not faded. Montaut's lithographs are always popular with collectors and have been reproduced many times in more recent advertisements. They occasionally can be purchased for less than $500.

Pre–World War I poster art advertising automobile shows is also very collectible. In the early days of the automobile, Leyendecker achieved fame with his illustrations involving

Photo album, artist signed cover, Esso gas stations, $15.

Playing cards, Michelin Tyres, replica of Montaut racing print, $20.

Print, Oldsmobile Runabout, 1901, Elminger, $10.

the new automobiles of the day. One of the most popular appears on the cover of the January 21, 1905, edition of *Collier's*. This was a special New York Auto Show issue, with the cover featuring a 1905 Mercedes with Madison Square Garden in the background. The Mercedes Leyendecker sketched was unusual, as it had been assembled in the United States. Some of the parts were actually manufactured at a Mercedes plant in Long Island, New York.

Art buffs sometimes refer to the time between World War I and World War II as the "golden age of illustration." During this time, well-known American artists produced automobile-related cover art for popular magazines. The magazine publishers were happy to comply with the automakers' request for special automobile issues, as the manufacturers were generous in purchasing advertising space. Original cover art is difficult to find, but often these covers or advertisements were reproduced in poster form for public sale. Automobile and train enthusiasts alike enjoy William Harnden Foster's 1910 Oldsmobile advertisement. This famous picture shows a 1910 Oldsmobile Limited racing alongside the New York Central's crack Twentieth Century Limited passenger train. Foster's ad has been reproduced often and recently, so buy with care.

In the 1920s, John Held, Jr., became known for his caustic portrayal of young people. His caricatures of flappers and their beaux nearly always involved an automobile, usually a stripped-down roadster. His amusing drawings reflecting the rapidly changing mores of the times and our increasing dependence on the motorcar appeared on many magazine covers of the 1920s.

Cartoonists were the first to lampoon those newfangled motorized wagons. Editorial cartoonists, wary of change, warned the public of the dangers of the automobile. Later, *New Yorker* cartoonist Peter Arno would more

gently poke fun at motorists and their fascination with all things automotive.

Any listing of modern automotive artists is incomplete without a mention of Tad Burness, whose *Auto Album* gave us wonderful line drawings of antique and collectible automobiles, along with information about list prices, the wheelbase, and popularity, and has entertained generations of car lovers. Tad Burness' *Auto Album* appeared in Sunday comic strips for many years. He is now semi-retired and *Auto Album* appears weekly in *AntiqueWeek*. Arthur Fitzpatrick and Van Kaufmann did a series of more than two hundred advertisements for Pontiac. Fitzpatrick, known for his detailed automobile illustrations, handled the cars while Kaufmann, a former Disney illustrator, did the backgrounds. From 1959 to 1971, their advertisements for the wide-track Pontiac dominated the magazines. After World War II, automobile advertising executives and magazine publishers began using photographs in automobile ads and on their magazine covers. Some years later, in the 1960s, photos were almost exclusively used in automobile advertising, ending more than fifty years of wonderful illustrations.

Photographers have lamented the fact that their work is often relegated to craft status rather than being considered an art form. Admittedly, some automotive photography can be rather dull. Factory photographs are not particularly creative, but they offer a wealth of information to the restorer. Such details as upholstery patterns, body and wheel pinstriping, paint schemes, and trim and accessories are detailed in factory photos. Photographers of automobile advertising layouts, though, have been quite imaginative and original.

Some of the most memorable photography in our automotive history are the depression-era photographs taken by the Farm Security Administration (FSA). The FSA employed Roy Stryker and a team of seasoned photographers, including Marion Post Wolcott, Arthur Rothstein, Russel Lee, and Jack Delano. Their assignment was to photograph roadside America, for at that time we were a nation on the move. Poignant photos show families traveling the United States, seeking a better life with all their possessions straped to an old Model T.

Postcard artists and photographers have chronicled American roadside history through their images of old garages, gas stations, automobile dealerships, and motels. Factory photos that detail make and model changes from year to year are also collected.

It is still possible to accumulate a nice collection of 1900s to 1930s magazine covers. Original cover art is very rare, and most of it already resides in museums or private collections. Early copies can cost hundreds of dollars, but for a few dollars, you can buy an entire magazine of the era. The cover itself will look great framed, and you can also utilize some of the advertisements inside the magazine. If you don't want to destroy an old magazine that is in very good condition, the entire copy can be matted and framed.

For many years, some art dealers looked down upon the art of the car. In 1947, that began to change. Halsey Davidson, best known for his automotive advertising illustrations, helped organize the first automotive-related art exhibition at the Detroit Art Institute. Currently, there are many galleries that specialize in automotive art; automotive art shows, to the delight of the collector, are becoming more common.

Today's automotive artists are organized. The Automotive Fine Arts Society represents the interests of the artists, and the society's highest honor is the Peter Helck Award, named after one of America's best-loved automotive artists and writers. The best automotive artists are the men and women who love the automobile hobby and are familiar with

Print, Stan Cline, 1950s giveaways, 1950s Texaco gas station scene, $5.

Print, Stan Cline, 1950s giveaway, 1930s 76 gas station scene, $5.

automotive history. It is also necessary to have an eye for the details that set each model apart and to be aware of its handling characteristics at events.

Many car lovers believe the classic automobile itself is a work of art. For such enthusiasts, the sight of a pink 1959 Cadillac cruising down the highway is poetry in motion, the perfect example of American folk art.

Automotive art is often one-of-a-kind art, making pricing difficult. Auction prices are determined by condition, by the popularity of the artist, and by how much the buyer wants a particular piece.

Bricklin, design illustration, mounted and framed with a letter of documentation, 26″ by 36″, color, $1,500

Christy, Howard Chandler, *The Motorist*, 1922, 39″ by 29″, $27,500

Clark, David, "33 Ford Coupe," 15″ by 21″ print, signed and numbered, 1993, $20

Comstock, Chester, Bronze eagle sculpture, commissioned by the Buick Division of General Motors, signed and dated 1982, one of 16 "artist's proofs," $600

Evans, Walker, "Joe's Auto Graveyard, Pennsylvania," 1936 photograph, 8″ by 10″, modern Farm Security Administration prints are available from the Library of Congress, about $20

Falter, John, *Trick or Treat*, oil on board, 17½″ by 15″, 1962 ad for Goodyear Tires, $1,700

Frank, Robert, best known for his photographs of 1950s automobiles and American daily life at the time; prices are $500 to $1,000, as the negatives are retired and no future prints will be made

Gamy, *Peugot at Indianapolis*, 1913, hand-colored lithograph, 17½″ by 35″, $1,000

Hamilton, Richard, *Hommage/Chrysler Corporation*, 1957, print, $1,800

Helck, C. Peter. Look for original illustrations Helck did for Chevrolet and Mack Trucks; he is best known for his early racing scenes.

Hershey, Franklin Quick, lithography of a 1930s painting of Murphy-bodies Duesenberg, 1 of limited edition of 1,000, $200

Ishmael, Woodi, Mack Truck advertisement, watercolor, 12″ by 19½″, signed Woodi, $175

Lange, Dorothea, *Texas Drought Refugees, August, 1936*, poor family in Model A, modern print from original negative, $25

Leyendecker, Joseph C., *Automobile Number*, oil on canvas, 19¼″ by 28″, cover for *Collier's* January 6, 1917, fashionable lady with auto, $25,000

Parrish, Maxfield

　Calendar for Dodge, 1921, in original box, $60

　The Peerless Girl, 13″ by 26″, poster for Peerless Motor Car Company, $85

Prince, William M., *Dodge Brothers Coach*, oil on canvas, 19″ by 27½″, one of a series of ads for Dodge cars, $700

Ragan, Leslie, *Cars and Sailboats*, watercolor, 19″ by 22″, *Nash* magazine advertisement, $2,200

Rockwell, Norman, *The Auto Repairman*, oil en graisaille on canvas, 11⅞″ by 17″, original art for Raybestos Brake Service advertisement, $8,800

Rosenquist, James

　Hey! Let's Go For a Ride, lithograph, numbered sixty-eight out of seventy-five, $2,500

　I Love You with my Ford, numbered print, $2,200

Sheeler, Charles, series of 1927 photographs of Ford's River Rouge plant in Michigan, prices

Norman Rockwell print, "The Street Will Never Be the Same," commissioned by Ford, $15.

Painting, Peter Helck, "Setting a Furious Pace," 1971. Courtesy of The Raymond E. Holland Automotive Art Collection.

vary from $500 to $1,200 as Sheeler's work rarely comes on the market

Stieglitz, Alfred, "Hand on the Wheel," 1933 photograph, $800

Stone, Gilbert, *Cale Yarborough at the Daytona 500*, 1970, acrylic, 24″ by 25½″, original artwork for story illustration in *Sports Illustrated*, $800

Tepper, Saul, look for his original illustrations used for Packard and Mobil Oil Company advertising, $500 to $1,500

Unknown artist, 1965 Ford taxi painting, hung in Ford's Manila, Phillipines, lobby for many years, 28″ by 38″, $500

Werntz, Carl N., *Old Days, Old Motor Cars*, oil on board, $700

Wood, Grant, *Death of Ridge Road*, auto accident, limited edition print, $2,000

Dream Thunderbird, show car concept, original drawing from Ford Motor Co., $125.

Youngblood, Kenny, *Swamp Rat XXX* print, Don Garlits's famous dragster, signed and numbered, $40

5

Auto Show Memorabilia

The Grand Salon in Paris was an extravaganza at which French automakers introduced their latest models to the motoring public. The success of the Paris show inspired members of the Automobile Club of America to stage a similar show in New York City's Madison Square Garden. The club, supported by promises of participation from the automakers, announced its intention to hold the first all-automobile show in the United States in November 1900. This was the beginning of the esteemed New York Auto Show, which went on to become a fall tradition.

In an effort to scoop the New York automotive hobbyists, a Chicago newspaper announced that it would sponsor an all-automobile show in July 1890. It planned a five-hundred-vehicle parade and various competitions, including a ladies' race, a backward race, an obstacle course, and other tests of driving skills. These events were made all the more challenging by several days of heavy rain preceding the event. Few spectators, and even fewer participants, showed up for what may have been America's first organized mud bog competition. In spite of this unfortunate beginning, the Chicago Auto Show went on to become a major event for automakers and their customers.

Although the New York group was worried

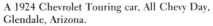
A 1924 Chevrolet Touring car, All Chevy Day, Glendale, Arizona.

by the lack of attendance at the Chicago show, it went on with its plans for an elegant event at the premier show in November 1900. Automakers displayed more than three hundred new vehicles. Gasoline, electric, and steam-powered vehicles were shown to prospective buyers and competed with one another in various events. The New York show was a huge success, attracting thousands of spectators. It had started out as a club event, entertaining the high-society types of the day, who were the only ones who could afford a motorcar at that time. However, these shows quickly became established as a manufacturer's show, where all of the automakers could display their products and where all of the citizens could go to purchase that dream car or to simply window-shop.

It was also a place where automakers could display the fantastic one-of-a-kind show vehicles that they could never afford to put into production. Studebaker, at the 1916 National Automobile Show, exhibited a gold chassis valued at more than $25,000 then. Photographs of these elaborate displays, advertising posters, and literature handouts from these early shows are popular with collectors today. Automakers made a concerted effort to win over the ladies by handing out sewing kits, recipe booklets, and compacts in their efforts to sell cars at these shows.

Along with the yearly auto shows held to

Chrysler World's Fair ashtray, 1933 Century of Progress, $45.

introduce new models, the world's fairs and expositions also offered the automobile manufacturers and auto accessory firms a chance to meet the public and display their new products. Although all of the expositions since the 1876 Philadelphia Centennial have given us advertising collectibles and souvenirs, none can match the quantity generated by the 1933 Chicago Century of Progress Exposition and the 1939 New York World's Fair. Collectors estimate that the 1939 World's Fair generated more than twenty-five thousand different souvenir items, many of them auto-related.

Collectors will find that souvenirs from the World's Fairs were often carefully preserved and turn up with regularity at antiques meets and paper collectible shows.

For the Century of Progress Exposition, Pierce Arrow built five special automobiles, highly streamlined versions that it named the "Silver Arrow." Three of these cars are known to exist today. Studebaker went one step further, creating a gigantic model of its 1934 Land Cruiser. It measured eighty feet long, twenty-eight feet tall, and thirty feet wide. Below this humongous automobile replica was a theater that showed films about the new Studebaker models. Nash automobiles were displayed in the "Nash Tower of Values," a clear glass-lighted tower in which new Nash automobiles moved up, around, and back down twenty-four hours a day. Chrysler claimed to have the largest private exhibit at the Century of Progress Exposition. Its display covered seven acres of the grounds. Famous race driver Barney Oldfield and his student drivers took fair patrons for an exciting drive around the Chrysler test track. At these displays, automakers gave away or sold hundreds of different souvenirs, sales catalogs, maps of the fairgrounds, and schedules of events.

The automobile memorabilia from these fantastic fair exhibits varies from recipe books, advertising, and postcards to giveaways, such

One of the last woodies, 1956 Ford Country Squire on display at Fabulous Fifties Day, Tempe, Arizona.

as needle packets, ashtrays, combs, and yardsticks. It is collected by auto lovers as well as by World's Fair buffs.

The General Motors Motorama Shows of the 1950s grew out of its new model programs, such as the 1949 Transportation Un-limited Show. In 1953, the traditional fall automobile show was renamed Motorama and expanded, introducing America's first two-seater sports car, the new fiberglass Corvette. Also on display were futuristic show cars designed and built especially for the Motorama.

Chevrolet in full-dress mode with Continental kit, 1955, All Chevy Day, Glendale, Arizona.

A rare 1957 Cameo on display, photo courtesy of Grumpy's Truck Parts.

Sometimes these show cars proved so popular with the public that they were given a more practical treatment and then mass-produced. That model year's regular production vehicles at these events were often displayed on turntables, with their features and accessories demonstrated by beautiful models. The 1953 Motorama packed up after opening in New York City and traveled the country from Miami to Los Angeles. Although the show cost more than $4 million to produce, it drew about one and a half million spectators. This elaborate show continued until the 1960s.

Hoods up! A typical auto show scene.

Today's automobile shows are often commercial events, designed to sell new models to consumers. They offer an opportunity to obtain sales literature and flyers showing the new models.

Fans of the supermodified, one-of-a-kind show cars that used to be shown at these shows will find them at events sponsored by the International Show Car Association (ISCA). While some of the fabulously equipped cars seen are by local talent, many of the owners follow the ISCA circuit around the country, earning points toward the awards given at the end of the season.

Today, most antique automobile shows are sponsored by collector clubs. These events are usually yearly, with a judged show and swap meet. Often clubs will bring out their cars for the benefit of local charities.

Advertising posters, programs, and award plaques and trophies are collected from auto shows of the past.

Advertisement, Chevrolet Motorama, Waldorf
Astoria, New York City, January 19 through 21,
admission free, shows cleaning women eyeing
1956 Chevrolet Convertible, $5

Arrowhead, 1934 World's Fair, zinc arrowhead,
$25

Badge

    Buffalo Auto and Truck Show, 1913, nickled
brass, shows winged wheel and open cab
truck, $45

    Buffalo Auto Show, 1914, shows open touring
car, $50

Booklet, *Chrysler at the Century of Progress Exposition,* 4½″ by 6″, illustrations of Chrysler's new
sedans, $15

Lapel Pin

    Big Expo Auto and Truck Show, 1914, red/
white/gold cloisonné, $20

    Mason City Auto Show, March 1918, shows
touring car, blue/white, 1¼″ diameter, $35

    "Motor Shows Overseas Visitor," oval, red/white/
blue cloisonné, London, 1964, $20

License Plate, 1992 Bloomington Gold Corvette
Show, $15

Pendant, replica of Chrysler's 1971 Rose Bowl
Float, boxed, $20

Pinback Button

    Milwaukee Auto Show, 1920, 1½″ diameter, $10

    Philadelphia Auto Show, 1925, 1¼″ diameter,
$15

Promotional model, GM Mid-Century Motorama,
1950 truck, $150.

Car Show Trophy, best "Neat Ole Truck," $65.

**Barret-Jackson Auction bank, 20th anniversary, 1991,
$35.**

Rochester, New York Automobile Trade Association Auto Show, metal, 1921, $10

Postcard, shows Ford "Road of Tomorrow" Exhibit at the 1939 New York World's Fair, $12

Program

Boston Auto Show, 1915, $25

Detroit Auto Show, 1987, $5

Indianapolis Custom Auto Show, 1951, $10

New York Auto Show, 1910, $25

New York Auto Show, 1958, $15

Philadelphia Auto Show and National Antique Auto Show, 1949, $20

Promotional Model Car, 1992 Black Hills Classic Show, black ZR1, $150

Stamp, 1914 New York Auto Show, 2″ by 3″, colorful, $5

Ticket, 1916 New York Auto Show exhibitor's ticket, $5

Token

Chevrolet Announcement Show, 1990, bow tie on side, "The Will to Win" on reverse, $5

Ford, 1935 San Diego Exposition, nickle, $15

General Motorama, 1954, shows Corvette, brass finish, $10

GM, Dale Carnegie Course, presented December 1955, $25

Tray, metal tray, 1934 "Ford Century of Progress," 12″ by 17″, shows Ford Rotunda building, $85

Trophy, RROC, 1954, "Smoothest, Quietest," $75

Boston weathervane, tin, 1907. Courtesy of The Raymond E. Holland Automotive Art Collection.

Christmas plate, Harley Davidson, $300.

Watchfob, Haroun's Marmon Wasp, 1911 Indianapolis Winner, $150.

Flag, National Hot Rod Association Nationals Winner on display at Don Garlitt's Museum of Drag Racing, Ocala, Florida, $200.

Michigan bicentennial sample plate, $15.

Service station maps, 1940s, $10 each.

Service station maps, 1950s and 1960s, $8 each.

Greyhound sign, hardboard, hung in travel agencies and bus depots, 1960s, $25.

Yankee Side-Vue Mirror, NOS, $40.

Riley Brothers grease can, $25.

Monkey Grip Tube Repair Kit, $10.

AMT "3 in 1" Ford model kit, 1936, $60.

Revell's slot car set, $75.

6

Ceramic Items and Curios

The motorcar caught on quickly with the American public. Even those who could not afford one were fascinated by the automobile. While children asked for toy cars, adults purchased curios that were decorated with pictures of the "modern" automobile. Potters were quick to notice that their wares decorated with replicas of the motorcar were good sellers. Plates, cups, saucers, sugar bowls, salt and pepper sets, and ashtrays all received an automotive motif.

One of the first to use the motorcar for decoration was the English firm of Royal Doulton. From 1906 through 1911, it produced a series called "The Motorist." Plates, mugs, bowls, pitchers, and tankards were hand decorated with scenes depicting some of the troubles that befell the early motorist. There were eight different designs in the series, and the titles alone are entertaining: After the Run; Deaf; Room for One; Itch yer on Guvenor?; Nerve Tonic; A Horse, a Horse; Blood Money; and The Old and the New.

Another kind of china that is widely collected has a more humble origin. The heavy-duty dinnerware used in automobile plant cafeterias and executive dining rooms is a great favorite of automobile hobbyists. Much of this restaurant china was produced by American companies such as Hall, Buffalo, Shenango, and Syracuse. Ford's famous Rotunda was featured in green, along with the Ford script, on their dinnerware made by Shenango China of New Castle, Pennsylvania. It is possible to date such dinnerware by the logo used or by the manufacturer. The green script with the Rotunda logo was used through the 1950s. Syracuse produced the more modern Ford dinnerware in white with a gray Ford script in an oval and a gray band around the rim of the plate. This dinnerware ranges in price from $5 for small modern pieces, to more than $100 for plates from companies that went out of business during the depression. Larger pieces are more difficult to find. Company dinnerware is usually collected one piece at a time. It would be unusual to come across an entire place setting at once. Silver plate marked with an automobile company name or logo is also collected. Such well-marked dinnerware and silverware are quite easy to spot at shows and swap meets. You must know your logos, though. Shenango's Pontiac dinnerware is

simply a white plate with the red Indian head logo in a circle and a band of arrowheads around the rim of the plate.

As the automobile became more affordable, china and pottery featuring the automobile became more commonplace. By the 1950s, many Japanese firms were turning out hundreds of pieces of dinnerware decorated with early automobiles for sale in the United States. Figural vases, salt and pepper sets, and

Plates and steins, Royal Doulton, early 1900s, part of the Motorist series. Courtesy of the Raymond E. Holland Automotive Art Collection.

Plates and pitcher, Buffalo Pottery, early 1900s, part of the Roosevelt Bears. Courtesy of the Raymond E. Holland Automotive Art Collection.

planters representing vintage cars were also produced in great numbers. Such imported items picturing American automobiles are still reasonably priced today. They are often priced less than $20, unless they are marked "Occupied Japan."

Many times, ceramic curios have the look of a generic car or truck; that is, they may look like a composite of the many open cars made in the United States or just vaguely re-

Plaque, 1950s Japan, $5.

semble a squared-off 1930s sedan. Lack of detail prevents the collector from identifying it as a specific make or model.

American potteries even made figural automotive cookie jars. These are tremendously popular with auto hobbyists and cookie jar collectors. American Bisque produced the Cookie Truck while Brush Pottery made a cookie jar in the shape of an old open touring car. Hall China, famous for its figural teapots, offered an automobile-shaped teapot, striking in either cobalt blue or black with gold trim.

Decorative metal curios often depict the motorcar. Ashtrays, cigarette cases, match safes, and tabletop cigarette lighters were made. Watch fobs and jewelry with an automotive theme may be gold or sterling, with decorative diamond chips or other precious gems. Much figural cloisonné jewelry features the automobile as well.

Christmas ornaments in the shape of automobiles are very popular, from the earliest German Dresden ornaments to the newest limited edition. Hallmark provides car lovers with a new collector ornament almost every year (buy them for half price on December 26!). Their most recent offering for auto hob-

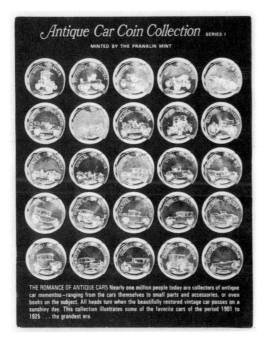

Franklin Mint, Antique Car Coin Collection, Series 1, $25.

byists is the popular 1964½ Mustang convertible. The Hershey Company has produced several tiny wooden vehicles driven by an elf. These are available at Christmastime by mail with proofs of purchase.

Hardest to find in recent limited edition series plates are the Harley-Davidson Christmas plates. These are produced in very limited numbers, usually only around three thousand pieces. Each plate is individually numbered, making availability extremely limited. Af-

Belt buckle, brass, 1956 Nomad, $15.

termarket prices soar when high demand exceeds supply.

What mention of auto-related curios would be complete without the Avon car? In the 1970s, Avon released a number of glass figural bottles in the shape of antique and classic automobiles. Decanters for men's colognes, the Avon bottle is scoffed at as being common by some yet is avidly collected by others. The Avon Collector's Club has a large following and some look upon the Avon bottle as a uniquely American collectible. They are a great way to start collecting on a budget, as they can be found for as little as $1 at yard sales or for as much as $150 for a very rare bottle. Avon collectors will purchase an empty bottle so long as the label is in good condition. Of course, the best find is one in the original box with its decal sheet intact. The boxes are colorful and well designed. Avon collectors also look for rare color variations. Of special interest are sample bottles, usually molded in clear glass. These are very low production and are thus priced accordingly.

Another collectible bottle is the ceramic liquor decanter. Although these were exiled from the collecting scene for some time, they, like the Avon bottle, are ready to make a comeback with collectors. Liquor decanters are generally released in limited editions and many are sequentially numbered. Liquor decanters are very detailed and are easily recognized as a replica of their real automobile counterpart. A 1957 Chevrolet Bel Air looks like a miniature 1957 Chevrolet Bel Air!

There are always new limited edition automobile-related items being issued. Decorative plates, ornaments, and figurines are available. Carefully consider the cost before purchasing a new item. Are they telling you just how many are being produced? Are the items numbered consecutively? Are they promising not to reissue? Some companies have been known to reissue after the first limited edition

Harley-Davidson motorcycle plush hog, $10.

run has sold out. You may have to wait many years before you can regain the price you paid for a new collector item. Few collectibles appreciate as quickly as claimed. With the same amount of money and some careful shopping, you can find an older item that is worth at least as much as you paid or possibly more.

Curios are fun to display, are colorful, and are still affordable. Of course, many older items, such as the Royal Doulton "The Motorist" series, will cost $300 to $500 for each piece, but you can still get a great Model T salt and pepper set for around $8!

Ashtray, metal, figural rotating trolley car in center, marked "Made in Occupied Japan," $20
Avon Car
 Haynes-Apperson, 1902, MIB, $6
 Pierce Arrow, 1933, blue/white, MIB, $10
 Thomas Flyer, 1908, red/white, MIB, $8

Bank
 Ceramic, 1959 Cadillac, pink, 1980s, $25
 Wooden old delivery truck, advertisement for bank on side, 1980s, $10
Bookends, black ceramic old open car, felt glued to base, Japan, 1950s, $18 pair

Universal battery ceramic ashtray, $10.

Ashtray, Champion Spark Plugs, race flags and their meanings, $25.

Ashtray, 1957 **Buick**, $20.

Avon Pierce Arrow, $10.

Bottle Opener, figural auto jack, chrome, 1920s, $25

Bowl

Black stoneware, 7½″ diameter, inlaid brass medallion says "Fifty years of Dodge dependability, 1914–54," $25

Ford Rotunda building shown in center, green band, Shenango china, older Ford cafeteria ware, $50

Oldsmobile vegetable dish, glove logo, Syracuse china, about 5″ diameter, $35

Bud Vase

Amberina glass, ornate bracket, 12″ high, $125

Carnival glass, Tree of Life pattern, $90

Button, decorative brass button, embossed with 1920s closed car, $10

Calendar Plate, 1909, lady in old car, months around rim of plate, $25

Candy Container

Fire engine, blue glass, $100

Glass, shaped like square 1930s-era sedan, plastic lid indicates 1960s, $15

Glass replica of an electric coupe, 4″ long, patent date 1913, $75

Candy Dish

Cadillac crest with wreath, gold/red/black, $15

Glass with lid, "Pontiac builds fleet excitement," red arrow logo, $15

Candy Mold, hinged, early automobile, about 5″ by 3″, $30

Child's Feeding Dish, 6¼″, Roosevelt Bears in old car, Buffalo pottery, $100

Avon Stutz Bearcat, $8.

Flower vases, Roseville Pottery, ca. 1906, part of the Tourist series. Courtesy of the Raymond E. Holland Automotive Art Collection.

Child's Tea Set, shows two children in a 1930s-era pedal car, complete tea set without original box, $150

Cigarette Case, silver, cloisonné face shows early race car with driver and mechanic, $75

Coffee Cup, United States Postal Service, National Truck Maintenance Center, Norman, Oklahoma, Frankoma pottery, $5

Compact
Brass, Chicago Auto Club Honor Member, raised red, white, and blue cloisonné logo, $25
Chrome, engraved with Art Deco–style roadster, $45

Cookie Cutter
Metal, shape of the Chevrolet "bow tie" trademark, 1980s, $5
Squared shape of 1920s car, 4″ long, $35

Cookie Jar
Bus shape, Disney characters in windows, $125
Cadillac, 1959, pink, 1980s, $25
Chevrolet figural, 1957, Applause, 1992, $50

Cookie Truck, marked USA, by American Bisque, $35
Touring Car, Brush pottery, $95

Cuff Links, New Departure Hyatt Bearings, Division of General Motors, tiny replica of bearing on each one, $20

Cup
Crown Staffordshire, England, shows 1903 Olds, $5
White milk glass, Esso tiger on front, $5

Cup and Saucer
Cactus scene, 1950s premium from Blakely Oil Company in Arizona, $10 set
Demitasse, Japan, shows 1890s motorcars, $5 set

Easter Egg, papier-mâché, printed scene shows the Easter bunny in duster and goggles delivering eggs in an open touring car, $150

Figurine, Meissen, open touring car, decorated with flowers and cupids, $1,600

Glass, shows gold 1964 Chevelle, dealer premium, $10

Hatpin, 2½″ diameter, brass head embossed with an open car, 6″ steel shank, $15

Lamp
Kerosene, miniature, orange ceramic base, white milk glass chimney, 5″ tall, 4″ long, stamped "Japan," $10
TV light, 1950s, black ceramic touring car, $45

Lint Brush, figural ceramic 1957 Thunderbird, lint brush underneath, $6

Liquor Decanter
Double Springs, Cale Yarborough, 1974, $75
Ezra Brooks, Corvette Mako Shark, 1962, $25
Ezra Brooks, Pontiac Indy Pace Car, 1980, $30
Famous Firsts, Bugatti Royale, 1974, $200
Famous Firsts, Duesenberg, 1980, $225
Jim Beam, Ford Model A Roadster, 1928, $35
Jim Beam, Mack Fire Truck, 1982, $70

Tie bar and cufflinks, early touring car, $25.

Lionstone, Johnny Lightning, No. 2, 1973, $75

Pacesetter, Camero Z/28, 1982, gold, one of a limited, numbered edition of five hundred, $150

Match Holder, ceramic, hangs on wall, decorated with early automobile touring scene, $45

Match Safe, silver plate, raised detail shows man and woman in open car, $95

Mug

Almelund Volunteer Fire Department, 50th Anniversary 1935–85, shows Russell Steam Engine, $15

Base reads "Truck Sales Honor Club, 1961," 1918 Chevy grocery wagon pictured, $25

Blue 1958 Corvette on front, GHC, Japan, $10

Colorful scene with 1827 Gurney Steam Coach, 6″ tall, McCoy pottery, $35

Occupational shaving mug, car dealer, name inscribed in black, $200

Occupational shaving mug, milkman, shows early (teens) delivery truck, name embossed in gold, $225

White milk glass, red and blue bicentennial logo, Chevy bow tie, courtesy of an Illinois dealer, 1976, $5

Ornament

Christmas, brown/yellow wooden trolley, mail-order premium from Hershey's, 1990s, by Kurt Adler, $10

Mug, "The Open Road," early motoring scene, England, $15.

Christmas, figural 1955 Chevrolet convertible, red and white, Mickey Mouse at the wheel, copyright © Disney, manufactured by Schmid, $25

Christmas, horseless carriage, possibly a Model

Mug, Gurney Steam Coach, McCoy pottery, 1950s, $35.

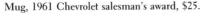

Mug, 1961 Chevrolet salesman's award, $25.

Mug, 1958, Corvette, GHC, Japan, $10.

Mickey and Minnie in their 1955 Chevrolet convertible, Schmid, $25.

T, blown glass, red and white, circa 1910–20, 3″ long, $150

Christmas, square-type sedan, yellow, 1930s, "Taxi" sign on roof, blown glass, $125

Christmas, truck, blown glass, about 3″ long, gold, silver, and red, $150

Paperweight,
Brass, 1963 Henry Ford Centennial, $25

Brass color, replica of 1902 Nash, celebration of Nash's 50th Anniversary, 1902–52, $125

Glass, photo of old car in bottom, $20

Pencil Sharpener, metal with antiqued brass finish, figural Model T, nice detail, Japan, 1970s, $5

Pin, lady's jeweled pin, figural old touring car, with pearl for steering wheel, $35

Pincushion, gold-colored metal open car, red velvet pincushion where interior of car would be, Japan, $15

Pink Pigs, Germany, ceramic pigs driving green car, 6″ long, early 1900s, $135

Pipe, Meerschaum, white carved pipe body, shaped like early automobile, red stem and wheels, $95

Pitcher

Eight glasses, "Put a Tiger in your Tank," Esso premium, 1960s, $75 set

Royal Doulton, 6″ high, Room for One, Motorist Series, $250

Planter

Ceramic touring car, marked "Made in Occupied Japan" in black on base, 5″ long, $15

Shawnee, red figural tractor-trailer truck cab, No. 680 on base, $25

Shawnee, trailer portion of above, No. 681, $25

Plate

Airflow Club of America, 1962–92, pictures seven Chrysler and DeSoto Airflows around club logo, only 250 produced, issue price $30

Black glass, kidney shaped with gold Chevrolets, Baby Grand, Royal Mail, and so on, painted on, artist signed "Z. Frank," $25

Black glass, titled "The Wheel and Transportation," 6″ by 9″, shows evolution of the wheel up to the 1940s, $25

Cream Ironstone, green rim, colorful red/green/yellow 1914 Model T Ford, by Brendan of Arklow, Ireland, $15

Gray Ford script, 9″ diameter, employee dinnerware by Syracuse china, $45

Harley-Davidson Limited Edition Christmas Plate, "Main Street, USA," 1986, No. 2,372 of 3,000, $425

Harley-Davidson Limited Edition Christmas Plate, "The Joy of Giving," 1987, 85th Anniversary of Harley-Davidson, No. 3,677 of 4,000, $350

Plate, Mercer Raceabout, $35.

Heavy restaurant ware, "Buick" script, $50

Mobil Oil, red Pegasus logo, 7″ diameter, $25

Potbelly Stove, ceramic, 6″ high, orange and black, says " '49 Nash, Hotter'n a Depot Stove," $50

Quilt, each block embroidered with a different brass era car, hand quilted, $100

Radiator Mascot

Dragonfly, signed R. Lalique, France, 6″ long, $5,000

Greyhound, signed Rene Lalique, France, 7¾″ long, clear with lavendar tint, $1,800

Sparrow, signed Rene Lalique, France, 5¾″ long, clear and frosted crystal, $2,800

Salt and Pepper

Brass era cars, ceramic, brown wood-looking finish, $8

Ceramic, red semitruck, green trailer, 1950s, $12

Ceramic set, salt is old-fashioned tire pump, pepper is a flat tire, Japan, 1950s, $12

Indianapolis Racing Car, 1950s style, $15

Limited Edition Roadster Salt and Pepper Shakers, numbered, painted in twenty-two karat gold, $25

Metal Greyhound buses, painted blue and white, movable metal wheels, sticker says "Souvenir of Pittsburgh," $15

Plastic Model T Ford, driver and ladyfriend wearing dusters and goggles are the shakers, $10

Streamlined car, resembles Airflow and Airstream-type trailer, $15

Silverware, Ford script, silver-plate knife, fork, and spoon used in Ford plant cafeteria, $5 each

Spoon

Souvenir of Garfield memorial, Cleveland, Ohio, top of spoon is touring car, handle decorated with steering wheel, goggles, bulb horn, $35

Souvenir of Indianapolis, 1950s race car embossed on handle, $20

Stein, Mettlach, early 1900s, decorated with vintage automobiles, Germany, $1,200

Sugar Bowl and Creamer, creamer is figural 1965 Mustang, with sugar bowl trailer, 1992, Applause, $25

Teapot

Hall, automobile shape, Airflow, black, with gold trim, $150

Hall, streamlined automobile shape, Chrysler Airflow, cobalt blue with gold trim, $175

Tray

Coca Cola, "Roadster Girls," issued in 1942, shows two girls with old car, $100

Metal, reprinted with 1920-era Ford ad, $10

Whiskey Flask, 1920s, metal openwork protecting glass bottle shows old car and says "Cylinder Oil" in script, $75

7

License Plates and Related Items

Even people who do not intentionally collect automobilia probably have a few expired license plates in storage somewhere. Before the days of yearly state-issued renewal stickers, it was common to see rows of expired license plates decorating barn or garage walls.

Registration of motor vehicles began at the local level when towns, cities, and counties issued registration tags or dash disks to each vehicle operated within their boundaries. Some local governments required motorists to display their assigned registration numbers, although they did not issue a license plate. Thrifty motorists created their own registration tags out of whatever materials were handy. Numbers were painted on boards, cut out of bits of metal, embossed on a piece of leather, and sometimes even painted directly on the rear of the automobile itself. Some automobile owners painted elaborate scenes on their homemade plates. The results were so creative that law enforcement officials found some of these first personalized license plates too difficult to read. It was not long before the states made things easier for the police, as well as the automobile owner, by issuing a statewide license plate that was uniform in size, color, and design.

Local license plates manufactured before the days of state-issued tags fascinate collectors. A good example is the Florida plates from 1913 to 1917, when some cities and every county in Florida registered motorcars. Each municipality's license plate was unique in color, size, shape, and style. Variations like these make the collector's task a challenging but enjoyable one. Such plates issued before uniform state-issued registration tags are very much in demand with collectors.

Hobbyists consider the earliest license plates to be the most desirable, not only because of their age but also because of the low numbers used. In 1901, when New York began statewide registration, less than one thousand motorcars were registered. Obviously, a

1901 New York registration disk would be a great find. California began a statewide program of automobile registration in the same year. It also issued a metal disk that was to be carried in the driver's pocket or screwed to the dashboard of the automobile.

A few states used the owner's initials instead of numbers. This quickly ceased as the increasing number of automobiles led to duplication of initials among motorists. States converted to a state-issued number or a series of letters and numbers. Some of the earliest license plates were not dated. Dating came later when the government figured out that yearly registration would increase revenues. State registration did save the motorist money, though. Before this time, a license could be required from each and every city or town in which the automobile would be driven!

In 1903, Massachusetts became the first state to issue a uniform license plate. By 1918, all forty-eight states were manufacturing statewide identification plates for all vehicles in use within their boundaries.

At first, porcelainized steel was popular, but it was fragile and chipped easily. The more durable embossed metal tags introduced in the 1910s are still the norm today.

In the 1920s, states began to use license plates as free advertising for the natural attractions of their state. Whether this was an effort to increase tourism or just as a matter of state pride is not known. Later, the state logo or motto was added. Almost everyone knows that Pennsylvania is the "Keystone State" and that Idaho grows "Famous Potatoes." Decorative pictures were added, such as Florida's famous flamingo, Maine's lobster, or Georgia's peach. Today, many of these distinctive logos have been reinstated on modern holographic license plates. Such attractive current license plates will surely please the collectors of tomorrow.

During World War II, metals were scarce and many states experimented with fiberboard plates. Illinois license plates for 1943 were fiberboard made from a soybean base. Folklorists claim that the goats of Illinois thought these tags were delicious. After the war, a tremendous number of antique car clubs were formed. They lobbied for special licensing for their historic vehicles, which, in many cases, did not have the original equipment required for conventional state inspection and licensing. In 1949, Michigan became the first state to introduce a historic vehicle plate. Virginia's historic vehicle plates were replicas of the earliest small procelain-on-steel license plates. Most states use a list issued by the Classic Car Club of America to determine eligiblity for such plates. Today, many states offer even more specialized categories, such as street rod designations.

Many states now have "year of manufacture" licensing, which allows a historic vehicle to be registered with license plates dated the year of the vehicle's origin. Now many collectors are more particular, as they often need a pair of license plates for a specific year to match each old car they own.

Commemorative plates are always in demand. In 1976, each state and territory issued a special commemorative license plate to celebrate our country's bicentennial. These license plates are still available at a reasonable price. Searching out a bicentennial plate from each state is a nice way to introduce a child to license plate collecting. Tags that

Inaugural plate, 1981, $15 pair.

Inaugural plate, 1977, $18 pair.

celebrate an anniversary of statehood or those issued for a presidential inauguration are quite desirable. Sample plates produced for display at state licensing offices are another facet of the hobby. These will either read all zeroes or be lettered "SAMPLE." Personalized license plates are also considered collectible. While some folks like to collect one state or one specific year, others will collect all license plates with a specific number. This is definitely a challenge.

Besides the license plates themselves, there are related collectibles that appeal to license plate enthusiasts. Many small items that resemble license plates and are related to the hobby are available.

During and after World War II, the Disabled American Veterans (DAV) began distributing key chains with a miniature license plate matching your state plate for that year attached. The DAV did not charge for these

Hatpin, miniature license plate, $3.

key tags but did ask for a donation. There are several versions of the DAV key tag, ranging from 1¼" to 1½" long. While the earlier versions are all metal, later editions were plastic. DAV key tags are especially desirable in pairs, with the earliest being the most valuable. B. F. Goodrich Tire Company also gave out license plate replica key chains. These are rare, compared to the DAV tags, and are generally much more expensive. While pairs of the DAV tags can be had for $5 to $10, Goodrich tags have been seen priced from $30 to $100. Privacy laws in the late 1970s disallowed the DAV's access to motor vehicle registration numbers; thus, the key tag program was discontinued. Today, these small collectibles are very popular. They are fun to collect, reasonable in price, and appeal to those with limited space for their collections.

Goudy gum cards were issued in 1938 with printed replicas of the various state license plates. In the early 1950s, Topps also offered a series of license plate bubble gum cards. A set of seventy-five cards was offered from 1949 to 1950 and another similar set was issued in 1953.

Not to be outdone by the gum companies, cereal companies soon got into the act. Wheaties offered reflective license plate stickers in 1950. These were replaced by miniature metal replica plates in 1953. Later, Post Honeycomb offered miniature metal license plates for young collectors. These are now reasonably priced. License plates were offered as cereal premiums as late as as 1989. These editions have a rolled edge and are dated and often are found for much less than a dollar at flea markets. Earlier editions were also dated but lack the rolled edge. These flat, embossed metal plates seem more realistic.

Paper collectibles related to license plates include old driver's licenses, titles, and vehicle registration forms. Especially desirable are those for unusual cars, such as a LaSalle or an Auburn Speedster. Other paper collectibles include postcards, maps, and advertising. In the late 1930s, Shell gas stations gave their customers maps with a montage of license plates on the front cover.

In the 1930s and 1940s, some states offered souvenir postcards that showed a replica of the state's license plate for that year. A unique advertising blotter shows the 1947 license plates of our forty-eight states, Hawaii, the District of Columbia, and all of Canada's provinces. Alaska is not included, but the blotter is colorful and makes a great display item. It also lists how many passenger cars and commercial vehicles were registered in each state for that year. Nevada came in last, with only 35,230 passenger cars registered in 1947. Tennessee's plate is the one shaped like the state itself, bounded on the east and west by rivers, while Utah's license tag proclaims "This is the place." In the 1960s, Atlas tire ads showed the current license plates of each state in their magazine advertisements.

For some years, the US government published a poster depicting the license plate used by each state. Unfortunately, it has discontinued this practice. Perhaps public demand can encourage the government to start anew. It is unusual to find any of these posters in good condition.

New state designs in license plates, ranging from computer-designed holograms to the return of such popular state logos as the Georgia peach and Maine's lobster, have helped increase interest in the collecting of license plates.

License plate attachments, embossed or painted metal plates that screwed to the top of the license plate, were especially popular

Dealer plate, 1968, mint in envelope, $15.

from the 1920s up to World War II. They are enjoying new popularity today as decorations for classic automobiles. They were painted to advertise insurance companies, automobile dealers, gas stations, fraternal organizations, and the like. Reflectors were also a favorite decoration. Attachments touting tourist attractions and beaches are also collected. These are usually very decorative. For example, Florida cities and beaches often offered souvenir license plate attachments decorated with palm trees and flamingos.

Some license plate attachmens are being reproduced. Be wary of an attachment featuring a 1930s automobile and advertising an insurance company. It should be priced between $5 and $15 as a recent article. Also suspect is a white metal attachment with the letters "UMW," possibly meant to represent the United Mine Workers Union. There are just too many of these at shows, and they are all in "like new" condition.

License plate collecting is a colorful and entertaining hobby. It is easy to get into as reasonably priced license plates abound for the beginning collector.

Advertisement, Atlas Tires, 1962, shows all state license plates, two pages from *Saturday Evening Post*, $5

Attachments

Cat, looks a little like Felix, eyes and tongue jiggle as you drive, NOS, 1940s and 1950s, with original glassine envelope, $25

Fayetteville, 1956–74, shows building, does not give a state, $10

"God Bless America," red/white/blue letters, with American flag, $65

"Ray Hagen Chevrolet Sales and Service," black and white, with Chevrolet "bow tie" logo, $35

Marathon gasoline license plate attachment, 1930s, $35.

"Roosevelt for President," words in blue and
 white, red metal reflector, $55
Souvenir, "1955 Soo Locks Centennial," $45
State Farm insurance, shows generic-type late
 1930s car, probably a reproduction, $10
"Wisconsin Sheriffs Association," heavy brass

Cat, license plate attachment, NOS, $25.

License plate attachment, souvenir of Fayetteville, $10.

License plate attachment, $20.

Reproduction attachment, State Farm Insurance, $10.

 with six-point star, blue/white, NOS in origi-
 nal wrapper, $50
Blotter, advertisement for Dodge/Plymouth
 Dealer, shows 1947 license plates of forty-eight
 states, $10
Cereal premium license plates
 Arkansas, 1954, $5
 Nevada, 1954, $5
 South Carolina, 1989, $1

Blotter with 1947 license plates, $10.

Wheaties cereal premium license plate, Arkansas, 1954, $5.

California dash disk, 1915 registration, $50.

Wheaties cereal premium license plate, Nevada, 1954, $5.

Topps Gum Card, 1953, $3.

Dash Disk
  California, brass, 2″ diameter, no date, $150
  California, brass somewhat worn, 2″ diameter, 1915, $50
  Illinois, 1916, $60
  Indiana, no date, 2″ diameter, brass, $150
Gum Cards
  Goudy, State License Plates Series, 1938, Illinois, $8
  Goudy, Texas, 1938 series, $8
  Topps, complete set of seventy-five cards, 1949, $200
  Topps, complete set of seventy-five cards, 1953, $150

  Topps, State License Plates Series, 1949, $3 each
  Topps, State License Plates Series, 1953, $2 each
Key Tags
  B. F. Goodrich
    Michigan, 1939, $30
    Ohio, 1940, $30
    Wisconsin, 1940, $30
    Wisconsin, 1941, $30
  Disabled American Veterans (DAV)
    Matching Pairs
      Illinois, 1951, $8 pair
      Iowa, 1951, $8 pair

DAV keytags, 1960s, $2–$5 each.

Arizona, 1961, pair, $25.

Kansas, 1954, $8 pair
Michigan, 1965, $6 pair
Minnesota, 1955, $8 pair
Nebraska, 1960, $8 pair
Ohio, 1961, $7 pair
Pennsylvania, 1951, $8 pair
Rhode Island, 1954, $8 pair
Wisconsin, 1956, $8 pair
Singles
   California, 1945, $10
   Illinois, 1949, $10
   Iowa, 1942, $10
   Kansas, 1944, $10
   Massachusetts, 1949, $10
   Michigan, 1948, $10
   Nebraska, 1949, $10
   New York, 1942, $10
   Ohio, 1948, $10
   Pennsylvania, 1942, $10
   Wyoming, 1949, $10

License Plates
California
   1915, $200
   1939 World's Fair, corner rusted through, $10
Colorado, Bicentennial Plate, "Ski Colorado,"
   $6 each
Connecticut, 1911–12 era, undated, $150
Delaware, 1913, four digits, $200
District of Columbia, Inauguration, 1977,
   unused, $15 pair
Illinois
   1920–93, complete set, $600
   1938, very good condition, $25 pair

Illinois, 1939, pair, $35.

Illinois plate, 1937, single, $18.

Illinois "soybean" plate, 1943, $30.

Illinois plates, 1949, checkerboard aluminum, $20 pair.

Sample plate, New York, blue and yellow, Volunteer Fireman, $20.

1943, wartime soybean composition plate, fair
  condition, $30
Iowa
  Dealer, 1916–78, $45
  Leather, 5″ by 15″, $210
  1921 pair, excellent, $25
  1933 pair, $18
  1949, checkerboard aluminium, $20 pair
  1964, antique automobile plates, $6 single
Massachusetts
  1901 dealer plate, mint, $200
  1911 four-digit auto plate, $70
  1915, blue enamel, near mint, $300
Michigan
  Bicentennial Plate, 1976, reads "Sample," $12
  Dealer plate, 1916, $150
  Farm, 1961, $25
  1914, $200 pair
  Original wrappers, 1953, unused, $20
  Pickup Truck, 1963, $25
  Sample Plate, bicentennial, $10
New Hampshire, 1916–93, three porcelains,
  $600
New Jersey, 1911, mint, $120
New York
  Black numbers painted on white-painted
    metal plate, about 4″ by 12″, $160
  Black numbers riveted to fiberboard, metal
    rim, about 5″ by 13″, $160
  Porcelain pair, 1912, red and white, few mi-
    nor chips, $185
  Undated pair, 1910, $160
  Undated pair, 1911, light rust, $135
North Dakota, 1933, $25
Ohio, 1910, $195

Pennsylvania trailer license plate, 1957, single, $5.

Pennsylvania School Bus, 1969, $10.

Postcard, 1940, Wyoming, $5.

Pennsylvania
  Red enamel, 1907, near mint, $300
  Schoolbus, 1969, in original envelope, $10
Motorcycle Plates
  Arizona, 1971, $5
  Iowa, 1952, $35
  Minnesota, 1949, never used, $100

Wisconsin, 1925, $60
Postcard, souvenir of Wyoming, 1940, shows Wyoming's Auto Plate, with cowboy on bucking bronco, $5
Sticker, Wheaties cereal premium, 1950, reflective sticker, replicas of each state license plate, unused, $5

8

Paper Ephemera

Many collectors and dealers buy, sell, and trade nothing but automotive literature. Collecting automobile advertisements, sales literature, books, and repair manuals is a specialized area of our hobby. This history of the American motorcar has been well documented in the catalogs and advertisements published by the automakers and distributed through their local network of dealers. Elaborate showroom albums, sometimes leather bound, can document model choices, upholstery and carpet materials, and power train options available in a specific year. These are excellent reference works for the restorer, as an older vehicle has often undergone many transformations during its years of use. Changes in upholstery patterns, installation of an updated engine, or a new braking system are just a few of the "improvements" that may have been made over the years. Such changes detract from the automobile's originality, and restorers often turn to original sales literature and parts lists to determine how their vehicle looked fresh from the factory. Albums featuring popular automobiles of the 1950s and 1960s are $200 and up while older albums are harder to find and are more expensive.

In automobile literature collecting, older is better and advertising from very low production older vehicles is scarce. Less than ten thousand units produced is considered low production. The older the car, the more difficult it becomes to find original literature and the more the hobbyist must be prepared to pay for it.

As in other fields, reproductions abound, so be very careful. Older reproductions of owner's manuals, advertising flyers, and the like may have the aged look and feel of the original but they are not worth paying the original's price. Such is the case with owner's manuals. These small, informative booklets were often lost or suffered water damage, making it difficult to find an original one in

Conoco Touraide, 1937, $20.

good condition. For display purposes, a reproduction owner's manual will do just as well. These reproductions are exact copies of the original, although an expert might detect subtle changes in the quality of the paper used.

Some color sales folders and catalogs are also being reproduced. These are the small, colorful flyers still offered in dealers' showrooms for their new cars. They usually contain pictures of the different models available for that year but are not as detailed as the showroom albums. Color folders can be small handouts — just one page printed front and back — up to a fifty-page, 12″ by 16″ catalog.

Most automobile companies offered a shop manual to help owners repair their own car. Because they were well used, it is difficult to find an old, original shop manual that is in good condition. Common defects are grease smears and missing pages. Aftermarket manuals from Chilton and Motor's auto repair manuals (Floyd Clymer Publications) are collectible as well. Older versions of these general repair manuals often include such marques as La Salle, Nash, and Lafayette.

The *Saturday Evening Post* was the first magazine in the United States to carry auto advertising. Ads are cut from old magazines and newspapers and are usually sold in a protective plastic bag with a cardboard backing.

These can be creatively matted and framed. Until the 1950s, when photography finally took over, some of the most famous American artists painted scenes for automobile advertising. Old auto ads not only show the way the car appeared new but serve to document the life-style in the United States at that time.

While many old magazines are torn apart by collectors looking for a specific ad, early publications featuring the automobile are collectors items in their own right. *Horseless Age*, the first automobile magazine, was published in 1895, leading the way for countless others. Magazines have been avidly read by auto enthusiasts since 1895, when Charles Duryea wrote an account of the nation's first automobile race, which he won. Today's auto enthusiast is likely to collect custom car magazines from the 1950s and 1960s, such as *Rod and Custom.*

Automotive books are informative to read and to collect. Many libraries have quite an assortment of titles related to automobile history and development, as well as repair. There are specialty books that relate the history of nearly every make. Self-help books are also available for the do-it-yourself restorer.

Tell-all books offer revealing, behind-the-scene looks at corporate politics within the automobile industry. Books such as *Ford, The Men and the Machine* by Robert Lacy (Ballantine, 1987) do offer some insight into how Henry Ford built his automotive empire.

Many novels have been written about the automobile, for instance, Arthur Haley's *Wheels* and Anton C. Meyer's *The Last Convertible.* Some of the most entertaining are the oldest books about motoring, though many are no longer in print. A series for young people called *The Motor Boys* and *The Motor Girls*, presumably for young ladies, was written in the early 1900s. The adventures of these young folks in their vintage motorcars make interesting reading even today. They of-

Motor Boys series, $12 each.

fer a great deal of insight into the problems those early motorist encountered, as well as the behavior of young people at that time.

Postcards were the most popular method of communication during those early days of motoring. Early on, postcards depicted motoring scenes—races, tours, and humorous situations. Even Henry Ford's Model T was the subject of a series of comic postcards. Auto dealers often sent postcards that pictured their new models to prospective customers with an invitation to visit the showroom. Such cards are still sent out by dealers. Also collected are those postcards sent out as service reminders by dealerships and service stations.

Postcard collecting is a specialty in its own right. Most large cities have a postcard collector's club and have regular shows where postcards are bought, sold, and traded. Automobile cards can be found under such categories as advertising, transportation, and comic postcards.

Many postcard collectors specialize in a specific type of card. They may collect cards issued by auto museums, dealer advertising cards, or only cards featuring a certain model. Postcards vary widely in price, according to condition, age, and the desirability of the model car depicted. As usual, the postcard showing a top-of-the-line sports coupe or convertible will be considered more collectible

than one picturing a plain-Jane four-door sedan.

Collecting letterheads, envelopes, and other stationery items used by automobile factories corporate offices and dealerships is a relatively small part of the hobby of literature collecting. Letterheads picturing the cars themselves are most popular and the most easily dated. These items are colorful and are still very reasonable in price. More recent items are often available for less than a dollar. Not as common, but just as reasonably priced, are the paper cups, paper plates, and napkins used and given out by dealers. These were sometimes used for complimentary cake and punch or given to customers for their own picnics. These sometimes have a picture of the car itself or a corporate logo.

Sheet music appeals to the automobile hobbyist/collector more for the autos pictured on the colorful covers than for the song content. Some early covers were beautifully lithographed, and these are more desirable than the photographs of the early 1900s.

Today, records and audiotapes and videotapes are more common than sheet music.

Record with 1963 Buick Rivera ad, $12.

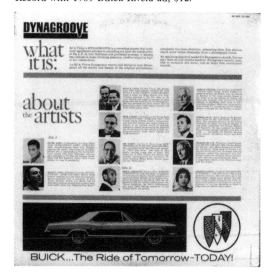

Through the 1950s and 1960s, dealers used filmstrips and records when training new salesmen and when introducing seasoned salesmen to the new models. These were gradually replaced by eight-track tapes, cassettes, and the current videotapes. In fact, television ads sometimes invite the consumer to write in for a free videotape of a new model car or truck. These are entertaining sales pitches and, at some future date, may be considered collectible.

Many new videotapes are available containing an assortment of old automobile advertisements. These compilations of old television ads from the 1950s and 1960s are entertaining because they give our children an idea of how we dressed, wore our hair, and entertained ourselves. Most people under twenty-one will laugh hysterically. These tapes are easily ordered by mail through hobby publications.

Collectible records vary from the salesman's pep talk to a 45 RPM (revolutions per minute) copy of "Little GTO." Tapes of old movies and television programs also afford an opportunity to watch old cars in action — often being wrecked beyond recognition.

It is also possible to order through the hobby publications videotaped coverage of nearly every auto event, including swap meets at Hershey and Pomona, road rallys, club conventions, and races. Perhaps video collecting is the wave of the future.

Stamp collecting, like postcards, is an area of specialization. Commemorative stamps featuring antique American cars have been issued in countries throughout the world.

Automobile companies issued stock certificates that were beautifully engraved and illustrated. It is this artwork, more than their collectible value, that makes the stock certificate desirable. Older issues from automakers long out of business, such as Pierce Arrow, Nash, and REO, are the most sought after.

Hot Rod Cartoons, 1971, $5.

Most favored are stock certificates that actually picture cars or the manufacturing plant.

Paper collectibles require some special care. They should be kept out of damp garages and basements and stored in a cool, dry place. Ultraviolet rays will fade paper memorabilia, so it should be displayed out of direct sunlight.

The most common place to find automotive literature is through advertisements in hobby publications and at antique automobile shows and swap meets. Visits to library sales and secondhand bookstores are often fruitful. When it comes to books, those that are out of print are the most valuable. Some limited edition volumes are selling for more than $100.

Many shop manuals and owner's manuals are being reproduced today, so check carefully with the sellers of new materials before paying a premium price for any literature.

There has been a recent rise in the popularity of full-size automobiles of the middle to late 1970s. Sales and advertising literature from this era is still easy to find and very reasonable.

Advertisement, magazine
- Corvair, 1961, color, 2 pages, $5
- Corvette, Silver Anniversary, 1978, color, $5
- Dodge, 1925, black and white, 2 pages, $10
- Ford, Fordor sedan, 1925, part color, $10
- Ford, 1963, color, 2 pages, $4
- Ford Mustang, 1964 ½, 2 pages, $4
- Harley Davidson motorcycles, 1951, black and white, $5
- Hudson, 1951, $5
- Oldsmobile Vista Cruiser station wagon, 1967, color, $3
- Plymouth Fury, 1961, color, $4
- Studebaker Starlight coupe, 1951, color, $4

Banner, paper, 1959 Rambler introductory showroom banner, $40

Blotter, "Drive A Ford & Feel the Difference," 1949, unused, $6

Book
- *The ABC's of Automobile Construction and Design*, 1943, softcover, published by Studebaker Corporation, $35
- *The Automobile User's Guide*, wartime suggestions for saving gas, published by General Motors, $15
- *The Chevrolet Story*, 1912–53, softcover, new models on cover, many black-and-white factory photos, $15
- *The Cobra Story*, 1965 edition, Carroll Shelby, $100

Chevrolet Story, 1953, $15.

Blotter, 1949 Ford advertisement, unused, $6.

- *Competitive Data*, 1934 Buick salesman's data book, hardcover, 107 pages, $60
- *The Dust and the Glory*, $200
- *The Great American Automobile*, 1957, John Bentley, Bonanza Books, $20
- *Jim Clark at the Wheel*, Jim Clark, $20
- *Motor Camping*, 1923, Model T in photos, lists United States campgrounds, hardbound, $25
- *Motoring Aboard*, 1908, Locomobile on cover, first edition, $60
- *Service Management*, 1929 Cadillac service manager's handbook, $100
- *The Treasury of the Automobile*, 1961, Ralph Stein, $35

Those Wonderful Old Automobiles, 1953, Floyd Clymer, $25

Turning Wheel, 1934, Arthur Pound, story of General Motor's first 25 years, presentation copy signed by author and GM President Alfred Sloan, $150

Wheels Across America, 1959, Clarence Hornung, $15

Booklet

Goodyear Blue Streak Racing Tires with prices, 1967, $75

Weber carburetor technical introduction, $50

Brochure

"Calling All Drivers," published 1938, Metropolitan Life Insurance, $10

"Have a Good Ford Summer," vinyl cover, suggestions for summer tours, 1972, $10

Holman and Moody camshaft brochure with prices, $25

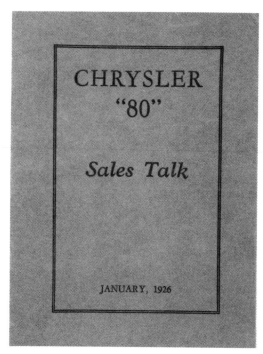

Chrysler "80" Sales Talk booklet, January, 1926, $20.

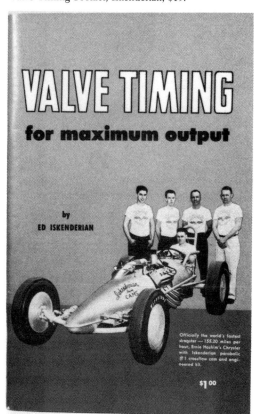

Valve Timing booklet, Iskenderian, $15.

"Chrysler '80,' Sales Talk" booklet, salesman's sales aid, January, 1926, $20

Bumper Sticker, 1970s Chrysler, "Rapid Transit System," $3

Business Card, Edsel dealer, late 1950s, $5

Catalog

Airflow, 1935, part color, 28 pages, $75

The AMX Story, 1968, color, $45

Bricklin, 1975, part color, 16 pages plus 24 × 24″ poster, $45

Buick (25th Anniversary), 1929, black and white, $95

Cadillac, 1927, 11 × 14″, 8 pages, $175

Cadillac V-16, 1938, part color, $160

Cadillac, 1964, color, $10

Cobra, 1965–67, roadster parts catalog with prices, $250

Corvette Silver Anniversary, 1978, color, $20

Cyclone Spoiler, 1970, color, GT Eliminator, $20

DeSoto, 1932, color catalog, $125

Duesenberg, 1929–31, black and white, 14 pages, Model J specifications, original binder, $250

Pep Boys catalog, $25.

Chevrolet full line color catalog, 1968, $10.

Plymouth Barracuda color catalog, $15.

Ford, 1965, high performance features, $100
Oakland, 1915, $90
Plymouth Barracuda, color, specifications, $15
Pontiac, 1938, color, printed in Japanese for export trade, very rare, $200

Comic Book

Woody Woodpecker in Chevrolet Wonderland, 1955, illustrated by Walter Lantz, $25

Corvette silver anniversary color catalog, 1978, $20.

Comic book, Disney/Arco, 1970s gas "crisis," $5.

World of Wheels, #23, 1968, Modern Comics, $2

Dealer Showroom Album

Chevrolet, 1957, paint colors, upholstery samples, and so on, $500

Chevrolet, 1970, includes Corvette and Camaro, with fabric samples, paint chips, and so on, $300

Folder

Cadillac, 1929, part color, $25

Chandler Royal 8, 1928, part color, $50

Chevrolet Accessory List and Price Schedule, 1955, confidential to dealers, reproduced, 3 pages, $3

Crosley, 1939, color, $65

Jeep, 1970, color, full line, shows paint and upholstery options, $5

Lafayette, 1934, color, dealer item, first year, $40

Lincoln, 1956, color, $20

Mercury, 1957, color, $15

Packard, 1954, color, $10

Packard Clipper, 1956, color, $15

Peerless, 1909, part color, embossed cover, $175

Stout Scarab, 1936, black and white, rare, $150

Instruction Manual

Cadillac, 1918, $35

Chrysler Four, 1925, $25

Ford, 1918, soiled, $15

Rickenbacker, 1920s, $35

Willys-Knight, 1920s, $35

Magazine

Automobile Dealer and Repairer, volume 12, #2, October, 1911, $20

Automobile Review, volume 6, #3, March, 1902, $25

Buick Magazine, October 1942, announcement of new models, $45

Chevrolet Friends, March 1952, $10

Corvette News, January 1977, $3

Chrysler Four Instruction Book, 1925, $25.

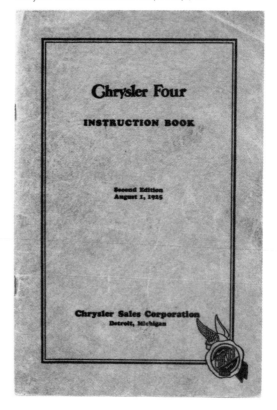

Horseless Age, volume 5, #10, December 6, 1899, $30

Motor, January 1932, Show Number, $20

Steam Motor Journal, volume 2, #12, March, 1909, slight cover damage, $30

Owner's Manual

Auburn Beauty 6, 1920, $45

Buick Electra, Le Sabre, and Wildcat, 1972, $7

Chandler Big Six, 1927, $55

Chevrolet Truck (reprint), 1957, $5

Ford Thunderbird, 1961, $15

Hudson Hornet, 1956, $40

Packard, 1934, $325

Plymouth, 1931, $15

Pontiac, 1927, $35

Rambler, 1907, $95

Rambler, 1956, $8

Studebaker Commander, 1941, $40

Paint Chips

Chevrolet, 1955, $15

Edsel, 1960, Dupont paints, $25

Pamphlet, 1966 Hooker Headers, $25

Photograph, factory issued

Diana, 1927, $25

Dodge, 1923, $10

Lone Ranger/the Dodge Boys, 1968, $5

Postcard, dealer

Buffalo Electric, 1901, Babcock, shows car, $50

Cadillac El Dorado convertible, 1965, $6

Chevrolet pickup, 1968, El Camino, $3

Chevy Baby Grand, 1913, OK used cars, $5

Ford Torino GT, 1969, $5

Nash Airflyte, 1953, $8

Oldsmobile Toronado, 1967, $8

Postcard, Route 66, 1950s, $6.

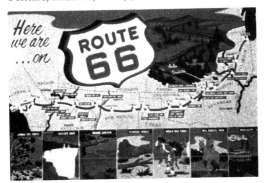

Rambler Super Cross Country Station Wagon, 1959, $5

Silver Anniversary Corvette, 1978, shows 1953–78, $10

Poster

Chevrolet El Paso Zone, 1936, Chevrolet used car Slug-fest, salesman's incentive plan, $15

Chevrolet Golden Anniversary showroom poster, 1962, 18″ by 32″, $30

American Motors Javelin AMX, 1968, shows AMX racing at Monte Carlo, showroom poster, 18″ by 23″, $30

Press Kit, 1981 DeLorean, four factory photos, fifteen printed sheets, folder, $150

Price List, 1916 Dort, parts and prices, $50

Salesman's Data Book

Cadillac, 1964, $125

Chrysler, 1956, with binder, $135

Sheet Music

Buick "I Love My Horse and Wagon but Oh! You Buick Car," $30

Buick, 1951, in original Buick binder, $50

McGurk Price List, $5.

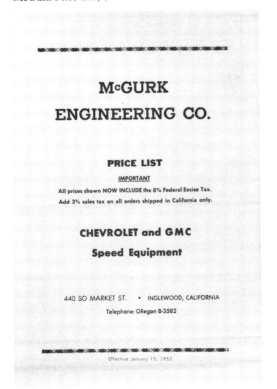

Chevrolet data book, 1951, $125.

"Dodge Brothers March," $15
Oldsmobile, 1967, $60
Shop Manual
    Avanti by Studebaker, 1964, $50
    Buick, 1936, $30
    Cadillac, 1952, $40
    Cadillac, 1959, $25
    Corvair, 1960, $20

McGurk performance bulletin, $10.

Texaco lubrication chart, 1937, $40.

    Corvette, 1963, $45
    Dodge, 1956, $45
    Lincoln, 1956, $45
    Mustang, 1966, $30
    Nash Metropolitan, 1955, $50
Songbook, 1964, "Sing of the USA," softcover,
    new models on reverse, including Corvette, $10
Stamp
    U.S. postage, $.12, shows 1909 Stanley Steamer,
        issued 1985, $.50
    U.S. postage, $.17, shows 1917 Electric Auto, is-
        sued 1981, $.75
    U.S. Special Delivery stamp, 1922–25, $4
Stock Certificate
    Four Wheel Drive Auto Company, 1918, $45
    Hudson Motor Car Company, 1954, pictures as-
        sembly plant, $15
    Kaiser-Frazer, 1940s, $10
    Smith Motor Truck Corporation, Virginia, 1917,
        $25
Title, 1932 Virginia Certificate of Title, Chevrolet
    coupe, $25
Warranty, Owner's Service Policy, 1955 Chevrolet
    Bel Air, issued by Murphy Motors, Richland,
    Washington, $8

9

Service Station Collectibles

Can you remember when filling your tank with gasoline was a pleasant event? Pulling up to the pump, you ran over a rubber hose and heard a resounding "ding" come from within the service station. Regardless of the weather, a uniformed attendant rushed out of the building. After politely asking how he could be of service, the attendant filled your car's tank, washed the windshield, and offered to check under the hood. Talk about the good ol' days!

As the use of the horseless carriage spread throughout the United States, the gasoline-powered internal combustion engine became the powerplant of choice, gradually easing out the steam- and electric-powered vehicles of the day.

This demand for gasoline resulted in the formation of numerous local oil companies, which drilled their own wells and produced fuel under their own name. Memorabilia from these small, independent oil companies is high on the want list of the petroliana collector. Many of these companies were in business only a few years before they were bought out by larger companies; thus, their names and logos vanished. Many of the smaller firms went bankrupt during the Great Depression of the 1930s.

The remaining few independent companies managed to stay in business until the gas crunch of the 1970s. Up to this time, service stations had continued their tradition of service to the consumer by pumping gas, checking the oil, and even voluntarily washing windshields. Neighborhood station operators cared about pleasing their regular customers, often giving out little "thank you" gifts with a fill-up. With the long gas lines of the 1970s, many changes in the way service stations treated their customers came about. Customer courtesies were dropped as station managers were forced to cut back on frills and personnel. Today, a full-service gasoline station is as hard to find as the proverbial needle in the haystack.

Just about anything related to, used by, or given away by the gas stations of yesteryear is collectible. Most sought after are oil bottles and cans, signs, and even gas pumps.

Old gas pumps, oilcan racks, grease pumps, and large signs are often used by collectors to create a miniature service station at their home. A replica of a gas station in the backyard makes a little larger display than most collectors can accommodate, and there are many smaller items available for lovers of petroliana.

Tins are at the top of most collectors' want lists. Quart oilcans, four-ounce "handy oilers," and one-pound grease cans are very popular, but just about any colorful tin that once held an oil company product could be added to a collection of petroliana. Tins decorated with unique corporate logos and slo-

Richlube oil can rack, $300.

Beeline grease pump, $250.

gans, such as the Hancock rooster, are very desirable. Cans with colorful graphics are more collectible than those with just a corporate logo.

In 1913, Gulf became the first oil company to offer free road maps and updates on local road conditions to their customers. These early maps clearly show how few roads existed for motorists before the interstate highway system was built. Free maps bearing an oil company logo were gradually phased out in the 1980s. They have since been replaced with map vending machines.

Mobil Lustre Cloth, $15.

Pencil or pen marks, tears at the folds, or water stains will detract from a map's collectible value. Maps from the 1910s to the late 1930s range in price from $10 to $50, depending on age, rarity, and condition. Those from oil companies that served a small, localized area for a short time are rarer and more desirable than are maps from large companies that have remained active nationwide.

Small handouts, such as banks, gas pump–shaped plastic salt and pepper shakers, or road maps, are particularly popular with petroliana collectors. They are always looking for figural banks, radios, and salt and pepper sets bearing the oil company logos that were presented to regular customers in the 1950s and 1960s.

Service stations gave away and sold several different types of banks. An opaque white glass bank, shaped like a baseball, was actually a Mobil premium given away at baseball games in the 1930s. These had a screw-on tin lid with a slot on it and a Bakelite base. Some of these had the Mobil flying red horse decal on both sides of the baseball while

others had the Pegasus on one side and a team logo on the other. A tin bank was also offered as a gift; it appeared to be an empty quart oilcan with a slot cut in the lid. Banks were also made from metal four-ounce oilcans and from the cardboard quart cans. One of the disadvantages of this kind of bank is that you can't retrieve your money without a can opener. If you find an oilcan bank intact, they are priced from $5 to $25, depending on age and condition. Other decorative banks are the miniature tin replicas of the gas pumps of the 1960s. These are harder to find than the oilcan banks and are usually in the $30 to $50 price range. These banks had a removable metal lid with a coin slot cut in it. They are of the same size and design as the more common A&P Coffee banks. These are thin metal and very prone to rust and paint scratches, so buy the best example you can afford.

The rarest and most expensive oil company advertising banks are the so-called Fat Boy banks. These are chubby vinyl banks, with a boy wearing a traditional 1950s service station attendant's uniform. Various oil companies offered these banks, and they are selling for close to $100 for even the most common logos. Similar to the Fat Boy banks are the Buddy Lee dolls dressed in a 1950s-style gas station uniform. These dolls are sought after by petroliana collectors and doll collectors alike. It is difficult to find one with a complete uniform, right down to the visored cap.

Miniature gas pump radios were also common advertising premiums. Most of these are the small, rectangular AM transistor-type radios popular in the 1950s and 1960s. More unusual are the round AM transistor radios shaped like an oilcan. These are a little larger than the four-ounce can banks and, again, are usually AM only. There are some larger radios shaped like the early tall visible gas pumps and decorated with oil company decals. Because these are AM/FM and because they are packaged in a very plain box with no service station advertising, we think they are an aftermarket item sold in department and specialty stores rather than a gas station. They are nevertheless decorative and functional.

Oil company advertising slogans often featured an easily recognizable mascot of some sort. Husky had its dog, Sinclair its dinosaur, and Esso its tiger. Advertising campaigns were enlivened by slogans such as "Save the dinosaurs," "Put a tiger in your tank," and Texaco's "Trust your car to the man who wears the star."

Esso and its related stations gave out a new gift with their famous tiger logo on it each month. Probably best known are the tiger tails that hung out of some of the best gas doors of the time — GTOs, SS 409s, Impalas, and the powerful Fords of the day all had tigers in their tanks. Also distributed to the customers were birthday candles with tigerlike orange and white stripes, shopping bags, pinback buttons, coffee mugs, cereal bowls, a pitcher with a set of glasses, and even plastic coat hangers featuring that familiar tiger face.

Many gas stations offered toys with their own logo, such as the Wen-Mac Texaco tanker ship offered in the 1960s. More recently, oil company banks by such companies as Ertl, Spec Cast, and JLE Scale Models are becoming hot collector items. Texaco has created a series of Ertl banks, bringing out a new edition every year at Christmastime. The 1992 edition, a beautiful red 1923 Kenworth Stake Truck filled with oil barrels, quickly sold out. The prices for the early editions keep climbing as collectors strive to complete the series.

Gas stations were at one time very competitive, often sparking gas wars in which nearby stations kept lowering their prices until it seemed they could not possibly be making a profit. They also sponsored contests offering prizes. Many of these contest forms, coins, and prizes are collector's items today.

Service station attendant's uniforms, award plaques, and yearly service pins are also collected.

Antifreeze Tester, Imperial gasoline, $35
Badge
    Humble Oil plastic name badge, red/silver, $15
    Indian Refining Company, name badge, $45
Bank
    Amoco four-ounce tin miniature oilcan bank, $15
    Cities Service, four-ounce oilcan, red/white, "From the heart of the crude," $30
    Conoco, tin quart oilcan bank, $20
    Enarco boy, gas pump attendant uniform, vinyl bank, sometimes called "Fat Man Bank," $95
    Gulf, cardboard bank, folds into gas pump shape, 1960s, $15
    Mobil glass baseball-shape bank, Bakelite base, flying red horse logo, given out at ballparks in the 1930s, $45
    Sinclair, plastic dinosaur, 1950s, $10

Quaker State cardboard bank, $5.

Mobil baseball bank, $60.

Texaco cardboard bank, $5.

Sunoco, gas pump–shape tin bank with lid, $35
Texaco No. 1, figural 1913 Model T, Ertl, $600
Wolf's Head, four-ounce oilcan bank, $15
Banner, Richlube, 1930s, canvas 3′ by 5′, reads "Safety-Instant Lubrication at Zero and Below," $110

V.E.P. tin bank, $25.

Blotter
  Atlantic White Flash Motor Oil, $8
  Red Seal Motor Oil, $6
  Sunoco Nu-blue, $8
  Tokheim Stationliter gas pumps, pictures pumps, unused, $8
Booklet, Magnolia Petroleum, 1938, "Mexico in Your Car," travel guide, $20
Bookmark, Richfield, heavy paper, shows logos of all service stations accepting Richfield credit cards, $5
Bottle Rack, Shell, holds about a dozen bottles, 1930s, $235
Bottles
  Imperial Refineries, quart glass bottle, $45
  Mobil red horse "Upperlube," four-ounce bottle, $20
  William Penn, quart bottle, $45
  Wolf's Head, quart bottle, $40
Calendar, Gilmore, 1947, California service station, $15
Candles, Esso tiger on box of orange/white–striped birthday cake candles, $15
Catalog, Bulko oil premium catalog, 1959, shows Lionel trains, Roy Rogers gunbelts, and other gifts available for buying Bulko gasoline, $15

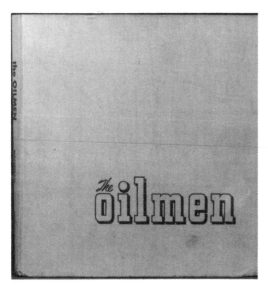

The Oilmen, Shell book, $10.

Clock
  Kendall Oil Clock, $135
  Phillips 66 tire and battery clock, $300
Coasters, plastic, Amoco logo and station address, 4″ square, $2 each
Coin
  Hyvis Oil Company, mileage-metered motor oil, chart on back shows which oil to use, $20
  Kendall Oil, "good luck," 1960s, $15
  Shell Famous Americans game, Shell logo one side, John Adams reverse, aluminum, 1960s, $2
Credit Card, Shell, 1934, $8
Credit Card Machine, Texaco, $45
Dinnerware
  Mobil Oil china platter, 12″ by 8″ oval, $65
  Mobil Oil oval vegetable bowl, 10″ by 7″, $65
  Pure Oil cafeteria stoneware, cup and saucer, $40 set
  Pure Oil cafeteria stoneware, plate, $20
Dinosaur, 12″ green vinyl dinosaur wearing service station attendant's cap and collar that reads "Dino," $75
Doll, Buddy Lee, hard plastic head, painted-on boots, molded hair boy doll, brown gas station attendant uniform, shirt, pants, cap, Phillips 66 orange/black patch, $300
Eyeglass cleaning tissues, cardboard covers shaped like quart Chevron RPM oilcan, $5

First-Aid Kit
  Mobil, flying red horse, glovebox size, $35
  Shell, brown tin with yellow Shell logo, full contents, hung in service station in the 1950s, $75
Game, Amoco Mileage Game, board game, with Amoco logo, 1971, $15
Gas Pump, Fry No. 17, five-gallon visible pump, $1,300
Gas Pump Globe
  Cities Service Coolmotor, shamrock shape, $450
  Conoco, $200
  Dixie Blue, $350
  Dixie Ethyl, $250
  DX Marine (shows boats), $450
  Speedwing globe, plastic with glass insert, $150
  Texaco, $350
  Tydol, milk glass, $275
Gas Pump Sign
  Atlantic Imperial gas pump sign, $40
  Ethyl, 8″ round porcelain sign, $35

Shell first aid kit, $75.

Mobil Regular, porcelain, 12″ by 14″, $65

Sky Chief Supreme pump sign, $60

Glasses, Socony, flying red horse logo, set of eight, $80

Glasses and Pitcher set, Esso premium, glass with "Put a tiger in your tank" printed in several different languages, $100 set

Handy Oiler, four-ounce household oil

Archer, Indian with bow logo, $25

Conoco Handy Oiler, green/white tin, red triangle logo, $15

Esso, three mint handy oilers in gift box, cover shows map of United States and "Happy Motoring" oil-drop character, $50

Phillips 66 Handy Oiler, $15

Hat

Kendall Oil, mechanic's cap, souvenir of 1939 World's Fair, $25

Marathon, unused, mechanic's cap, reads "Marathon VEP Motor Oil," blue/yellow, $10

White Rose Gasoline, military-style cap with leather band and brim, $175

Horseshoes, two plastic toy horseshoes, 1960s Gulf Oil advertising premium, $5 pair

Ice Scraper, Ashland Oil Company, early 1950s, $3

Key Chain

Enco Happy Motoring Key Club, tiger

Signal gas pump, $450.

Shell gas pump, restored, $525.

Phillips 66 gas pump, restored, $450.

DX Mini gas pump, $400.

Trio of handy oilers, $15 each, $50 for set.

embossed on one side, address for lost keys on reverse, $5

Peter Penn, "The Aristocrat of Lubrication," red/white plastic, $15

Shell, 50th Anniversary, Wilmington refinery, 1923–73, embossed with refinery and Shell logo, $25

Letter Opener, Exxon metal opener, red/white/blue logo reads "Employee Safety Award" one side, "Attendance Award" on reverse, $10

License Plate Attachment, Marathon, shows runner in center reflector and slogan, "Best in the Long Run," fair condition, $35

Lighter

Cities Service, 1950s flat-style lighter, Crown/Japan, MIB, $15

Shell Zippo cigarette lighter, $25

Speedway "79", red/blue/silver, $25

Standard flame logo on Zippo slimline lighter, $25

Lock, Conoco brass padlock, no key, $15

Lubrication Chart

Essoleum Lubrication Guide, 1937, $40

Hancock Lubrication Chart, 1952, $25

Texaco Lubrication Chart, 1937, $40

Magazine

The Conoco Magazine, November 1931, $12

Super Service Station, 1930s, $8

Texaco Lubrication Magazine, September 1946, $6

Map

Associated/Tidewater, colorful flying A Station on cover, 1940s, $10

Barnsdall, 1940s, twelve-state set, $200

Standard Oil Zippo lighter, $25.

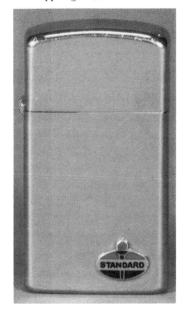

Carter, 1957, North and South Dakota, $6

Frontier Gas, 1930s, $15

Marathon, runner logo, 1961, $5

Pure Oil Pathfinder Map, 1930s Century of
Progress, colorful, $15

Veltex/Fletcher Oil, Washington/Oregon, 1946,
$12

Map Rack, Cities Service, small countertop size,
$35

Matchbook

Citgo, 1960s-era, Pennsylvania service station, $2

Clark Super Gas, shaped like gas pump globe,
$6

Husky, shows dog, 1950s era, $3

Matches, Skelly miniature oilcan matches, $7

Money Clip, brass, shield-shaped Phillips 66 logo,
$35

Needle Book, Linco Penn Motor Oil, $15

Oil Barrel Tap, Shell embossed logo, $125

Oil Change Reminder Tag

"Franklin Quality Oils," 3″ metal oval, screws to
dash or firewall, pictures Ben Franklin with
oilcan, $50

"Golden Shell," Shell logo one side, room to
write date and mileage on other side, hangs
from rearview mirror, $15

Paper Cup, Socony, flying red horse on cup, $2

Patch

Kendall, the 2,000-mile oil, 3″ round, $5

Shell Wings Oil Company, 3″ by 14″, $8

Skelly, 2″ by 2″, $4

Westland, 2½″ round shirt pocket patch, buffalo
logo, $5

Pencil

Mechanical, metal miniature oilcan top contains
eraser

Kendall, $15

Opaline, $15

Skelly, $15

Wolf's Head, $15

Mechanical, metal with clear plastic oil-filled

top contains miniature RPM oilcan, California Oil Company, $25

Texaco oilcan floating in oil-filled top, $25

Wooden, unused, "The Texas Company"
(Texaco), $3

Pin

Oil, Chemical and Atomic Workers International Union, 10 karat gold, oil well logo, $35

Phillips 66 Marketing Team, no date, $25

Shell, five-year safe driver pin, gold, 1920s, $100

Shell, thirty-five-year service pin, three dia-
monds, gold, $150

Standard Oil, gold, thirty-five-year service pin
with diamond, $95

Union Oil Company, 1934 shield with torch,
gold, two rubies, $150

Placemat, vinyl, Gulf Oil/Disney characters, $10

Plaque, Tidewater Flying A bronze wall plaque, 9″
by 11″, $175

Plate, 6″ sandwich plate, Mobil red pegasus, $20

Playing Cards

Lane Wildcat Wells, shows oil rigs, mountain

Gilmore hat pin, $3.

RPM pencil, $25.

Esso playing cards, $15.

Phillips 66 salt and pepper shakers, $35.

setting, double deck with original box, $20

Phillips 66 Service Station, 1960s, shows logo and gives address and phone number, $10 double deck

Pocketknife, Conoco red triangle logo, Nebraska dealer, $20

Puzzle

Signal Oil Company, Tarzan Radio Show puzzle, 1930s, $75

Vicolized Gasoline, shows 1928 Packard, color, $60

Radio

Amoco, gas pump replica, square transistor type, AM, $40

Sinclair, gas pump replica, plastic replica of old visible pump, AM/FM, $50

Salt and Pepper

Conoco, plastic gas pumps, $40

DX, plastic gas pumps, unusual, $100

Esso, plastic gas pumps, $50

Phillips 66, plastic gas pump replica, decals excellent, $35

Sign

Brice gasoline, two-sided porcelain sign, 40″ diameter, $375

Champlain two-sided porcelain sign, 4′ by 4′, $250

Cities Service Batteries and Tires, neon, $375

Conoco Minuteman, porcelain, $600

DX, single-sided porcelain sign, 4′ by 7′, $300

Esso with Ethyl, two-sided porcelain, $175

MacMillan, two-sided tin sign, pictures leprechaun, $375

Marathon, two-sided porcelain sign, shows run-

Mobil red pegasus, porcelain sign, $500.

Socony sign, $350.

Tape Measure, 4', Skelly diamond-shape logo, $35
Thermometer, Bell Oil Company, bell-shaped, 5"
  tall, original box, $25
Tie Bar
  Chevron pumps, "Treasure Island," $20
  Phillips 66 shield logo, $25
Tin
  Amalie 1# grease tin, 1960s, $15
  Archer, two-gallon oilcan, $35
  Coast to Coast, 1# grease tin, $15
  Flying A one-gallon antifreeze can, $15
  Heart of Pennsylvania, quart, blue/silver, red
    heart, $100
  Many Miles, black/yellow tin, red racing car,
    $250
  Oilzum, quart cardboard oilcan, $8
  Palocine Motor Oil, red/white, early 1900s, $150

Five gallon Texaco can, MIB, $45.

ner and logo, "Best in the Long Run," $350
Mobil figural Pegasus (flying red horse), 7',
  $800
Mobiloil Gargoyle sign, 1930s, porcelain, $500
Pennzoil, 16" sign, two-sided tin, "Sound your
  Z," $60
RPM porcelain, $375
Shell Lubrication, four colors, 3' by 9' porce-
  lain, 1935, $400
Standard fluorescent, double sided with flame,
  $300
Standard porcelain two-sided sign, 24" by 36",
  $200
Texaco Pacific Gasoline/Motor Oil, two-sided
  porcelain, 42" diameter, 1930s, $750
Silverware, knife, fork, and spoon, with Phillips 66
  logo, from Executive Dining Room, Corporate
  Offices, $30 place setting
Stock Certificate
  Bonanza Oil and Development Company, 1903,
    $15
  Fossil Oil Company, stock share, $10
  National Consolidated Oil, West Virginia, 1902,
    shows oil field, $25
  Red Arrow Oil and Gas, Arizona, shows gusher,
    1917, $15
  Stanwood Oil Corporation, 1945, $12

Pure Oil, ½ gallon, 1923, $75.

Texaco Home Lubricant, $15.

Richfield 1# grease tin, $35.

Quaker State metal oil quart, $10
Richfield 1# grease, eagle flying to right, $35
RPM Supreme one-gallon can, $25
Shamrock oil, metal quart, $20
Sinclair tar remover, half pint, $15
Sioux Motor Oil, 1940s, quart, arrowhead, $40
Tagolene/Skelly Oil, 1920s, half gallon tin, $200
Wolf's Head quart cardboard oilcan, $6
Tire Stand, metal, Flying A logo, $30
Tray, 1980 Coca Cola/Premier gasoline, commemorating the 100th Anniversary of Premier/Imperial gas, old gas station scene on brown tray, $25
Watch Fob, Polarine with polar bear on one side, reverse reads "Adds life and power to all types and makes of motorcars," $125
Yo-Yo, Duncan, Mobil Oil Little Ace, $60

Texaco underseat can, $125.

10

Racing Memorabilia

Before the turn of the century, automobile races were not speed contests but reliability runs to test the endurance of the vehicles. Still, some drivers could not resist the urge to compete. These "scorchers," as they were called, were firmly reprimanded by fellow participants and race officials.

The first automobile race in the United States was held in Chicago on Thanksgiving Day in 1895. Frank Duryea's American-built machine beat the European entries. In spite of the severe winter weather, the race was well attended. Auto racing has grown through the years to become America's number one spectator sport.

In 1896, the first organized race run on a racetrack was held in Providence, Rhode Island, at a dirt track originally built for horse racing. Automobile racing gradually took over many of the horse racing tracks around the country, as the spectators showed a preference for motorized vehicle races over the old-fashioned four-legged kind.

In 1904, William K. Vanderbilt, Jr., was said to be the richest man in the world at that time. He was quite a race fan and decided to sponsor the Vanderbilt Cup Races. He had his personal jeweler create a forty-pound trophy made of sterling silver and lined with gold. This first race was held in Nassau County, Long Island, New York, on October 8, 1904. A thirty-mile course on public roads was roped off and Vanderbilt's own newspapers provided a great publicity campaign.

Cross-country runs were common in the early 1900s. These racers were trying to make it coast to coast within a certain time frame rather than trying to outrun another car. Often these cross-country runs were little more than publicity campaigns mounted by a certain manufacturer to show the speed and reliability of its machines. Coast-to-coast runs against the clock still attract attention. The Great American Race, a parade of vintage vehicles driving coast to coast each summer, enjoys huge spectator support.

Hill climbs were a popular form of early automobile competitions, pitting driver and machine against nature. The Pike's Peak Hill Climb in Colorado has been held almost every year since 1916. Currently sanctioned by the United States Automobile Club (USAC), the twelve-and-a-half-mile "race to the clouds" is still held every Fourth of July.

It is hard to imagine the conditions that pioneer racing drivers encountered on unregulated country tracks. Rough road surfaces, spectators rushing onto the track, poor visibility, goggles smashed by flying rocks, and tires coming apart all combined to make racing a dangerous sport. As the cars went faster, it became apparent many improvements were needed to provide for the safety of both drivers and spectators. Most importantly, a better driving surface was required. Dirt tracks turned to mud at the slightest hint of rain. Board tracks made of wide wooden planks became common. After deplorable conditions in its maiden run in 1909, the Indianapolis 500 track was bricked over in 1911. This allowed the drivers a safer run, and to this day it is referred to as "The Brickyard."

The American Automobile Association (AAA) was quick to recognize that automobile owners were going to compete with one another regardless of conditions and set up a committee to regulate racing. Winton and Ford had built special machines specifically for racing that were not available to the general public. AAA felt that this was unfair to the many manufacturers who raced their factory stock vehicles against specially designed race cars and laid down a strict set of rules for factory-sponsored vehicles. The 1911 Indianapolis 500 was the first Indy race run under AAA rules and supervision.

With only a few years off during wartime, the Indianapolis 500 has been a Memorial Day tradition since that time. With this long history, Indy 500 souvenirs abound. Postcards, programs, autographed photos of drivers and their cars, helmets, goggles, pinback buttons, and fire suits are avidly collected. The Indianapolis 500 is still one of the most popular races in the country. Each year, we are treated to new cars, new drivers, and more memorabilia from which to choose.

In the meantime, the wide, sandy beaches of Daytona and Ormond Beach in Florida had attracted the attention of racing car drivers, owners, and manufacturers who wanted to set speed records. It was here that the "mile a minute" records were set and then broken again and again. Conflicting reports give credit to two great drivers in breaking the one-minute mile mark. Credit is given to Barney Oldfield, the famous racing driver, for being first to cover the mile in less that sixty seconds, with a time of 55.8 seconds in 1903. Don Wurgis is also given credit for breaking that record, also in 1903 at Daytona Beach. After the 1930s, land/speed records would be set on the salt flats of Utah and California.

Legend has it that stock car racing got its start with the souped-up machines necessary to outrun the law while transporting moonshine. Regardless, organized stock car racing got its start at Daytona. In 1936, the city of Daytona sponsored a race on the beach. En-

Indianapolis 500 courtesy card, signed Tony Hulman, $5.

tries were limited to stock automobiles rather than specially built race cars. Bill France, a local gas station owner, raced his 1935 Ford and finished in fifth place. France loved stock car racing, though, and after service in World War II, he promoted local races. Seeing a need for a governing body to keep racing safe and honest, he invited other promoters to meet with him in Daytona Beach. As a result of this meeting, the National Association of Stock Car Automobile Racing—NASCAR— was formed, and Bill France was elected president. NASCAR issued its first of many rule books for the 1948 race season. Today, NASCAR racing draws spectators from all over the world to races throughout the United States. The Daytona 500, also founded by Bill France, remains one of its most prestigious races.

Older NASCAR collectibles run the usual racing gamut—programs, driver's protective suits and helmets, commemorative flags, pins, and banners. In the last few years, die-cast replicas of current and past NASCAR race cars have been offered to the public. This collecting trend has taken off like wildfire. The announced retirement of one of NASCAR's most successful drivers, Richard Petty, has fueled speculation about collectibles licensed by him. Surely all the No. 43 cars will live on in stock car racing history, but there is just such a great quantity of Petty memorabilia available that there will be no shortage of it anytime soon. These new stock car collectibles are enjoyable and relatively inexpensive when compared to the hundreds of dollars asked for older toy race cars.

There is quite a lot of speculation concerning banks, die-cast cars, and car haulers representing the No. 7 Hooters car driven by the late Alan Kulwicki. Since his untimely death in a plane crash in April 1993, prices of Kulwicki's No. 7 car collectibles have gone up due to the demand by fans wishing to remember him and, sadly, by speculators want-

ing to cash in on a good thing. Use common sense when buying relatively new collectibles; don't get carried away by promises of easy money and fast profits.

Drag racing pretty much got its start on the streets. As soon as that first traffic light was installed, two cars probably tried to outrun one another the instant the light turned green. Being quick off the lights is still instrumental today, although electronic starting and timing equipment and modern safety precautions take much of the danger out of drag racing. Wally Parks, founder of the National Hot Rod Association (NHRA), is often given credit for taking drag racing off the streets and making it a reputable, fair, and safe sport.

The NHRA was formed in Southern California in 1951, at a time when citizens, concerned about the many accidents and deaths resulting from street racing, were asking for laws that banned drag racing. Drag races moved off the streets to abandoned World War II airstrips, and rules were enforced. Soon, smoothly paved drag strips opened, operating under NHRA safety rules. As a result, millions of spectators enjoy the quarter-mile racing each year.

Like stock cars, die-cast replicas of current funny cars and dragsters are available in the stores. Some increased collector interest has been noted in trading cards representing drag racers and cars both past and present. Older memorabilia from some of the most popular cars and race teams is not common. In the

Dash plaque, Manzanita Speedway, $3.

early 1970s, the Mongoose and the Snake captured the imagination of race fans and thus many toys featuring the Mongoose or the Snake were made. Most valuable are those representing the old front-engine dragsters. In fact, the Hot Wheels 1971 version of the Mongoose or the Snake is valued at about $150 each, mint in the blister pack. Mopar memorabilia from the 1960s Ramchargers racing team remains hot, as are window decals from defunct drag strips.

Look for Don Garlits memorabilia to increase with his retirement. Like Richard Petty, "Big Daddy" is a successful entrepreneur, and licensed memorabilia bearing either name or image is not scarce. Both men have had their automobiles enshrined in the

Don Garlits, 1980 press release, $10.

Smithsonian Institution's Transportation Collection in Washington, D.C. Garlits's Swamp Rat XXX dragster sits proudly alongside No. 43.

It seems that Americans are getting quite nostalgic about the days when almost anyone could afford to drive fast. In the good old days, everyone could afford to race a car. Fifty dollars would buy a "clunker" and a few friends could perform the modifications needed for drag strip or circle track racing. Safety requirements were minimal, and investment for these racers was small. Racing today is too often limited to those who can attract a big-money sponsor. Instead of going out racing, a fan now just has to be satisfied with his or her collection of racing memorabilia.

Prototype trading card, Don Garlits, $5.

Armband, Long Island Auto Club Racing Event Official, early 1990s, $75

Book

    Drag Strip Danger, Ross Olney, one of a series of books written for children about drag racing, 1972, $5

    Marlboro, *Salute to the 75th Anniversary of the Indianapolis 500,* 1986, many historic race car/driver photos, $15

Bumper Sticker

    Freemont Raceway, Freemont, California, red/white, $5

    Thunderbird, 1955–90, NASCAR Birds of Prey, $5

Calendar, 1960, photos of top stock cars and drivers, $45

Clipboard, "Chevy Racing," black plastic, red bow tie, $10

Cushion, souvenir of opening day at Ontario Motor Speedway, Canada, white with blue letters, logo, $50

Decal, Waterslide

    "Bonneville Salt Flats," pictures streamliner, $15

    "Champion Speed Shop," South San Francisco, dragster doing wheel stand, three colors, $12

    STP, checkered flag, Novi Indy Race car, 1950s, $25

The Complete Book of Stock-Bodied Drag Racing, $5.

Decal, Iskenderian, Daytona, 1957, $10.

"Valvoline Racing Oil, Participant, 1973 NHRA
　Spring Nationals," 4″ by 5½″, $6
Display Case, Autolite/Ford promotional plastic
　display, racing scene in plastic framed case, Pete
　Robinson's 1970 Tinker Toy AA/FD Dragster,
　marked "Limited Issue," $25

Flag, Checkered,
　Gilmore red lion in center, about 3½′ by 4′,
　　$250
　Mobil flying red horse in center, about 18″ by
　　24″, $150
Glass
　Indianapolis 500, 5″ tall, lists winners 1911–67,
　　signed Tony Hulman, $20
　Indianapolis 500, 1951, $20
Goggles, oilcloth, glass lenses, ties behind head,
　$75
Handout, Winston No. 1, 1974 Dodge built by
　Petty Enterprises, facts on reverse, $5
Jacket Patch, Indianapolis 500, May 25, 1986, $10
Key Fob
　Indianapolis Motor Speedway/Saint Christopher
　　Medal on reverse, unusual, $40

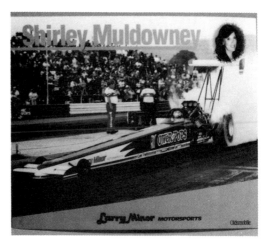

Handout, 1990s, Shirley Muldowney, $3.

Handout, Petty Charger, $5.

Jacket patch, Demolition Derby, $2.

Shape of 1950s-era Indy car, brass color, $35

Label, fruit crate, apples, shows 1930s race car, $10

Lapel Pin, gold, late 1940s, "United Stock Car Association," old No. 6 coupe in center, screw back, $35

Magazine, *TACH Times,* $6

Matchbook Cover, Champion/Lee Petty, $5

Medal, silver, Second-Place Winner, 1939 Chevrolet-sponsored Soapbox Derby, two participant cardboard ID badges, $45

Mug

Indianapolis commemorative frosted glass mug, Roger Ward shown, small metal race car replica attached to handle, late 1950s, $35

Indianapolis 500 commemorative frosted glass mug, wooden handle with miniature Agajanian racer attached, early 1950s, $50

Necktie, 1950s-style wide navy tie, gold vintage racing car, souvenir of Indiana, $35

Newspaper

Auto Racing "Foto Review," 1939, fair condition, $10

TACH, magazine of the American Hot Rod Association, $6 each.

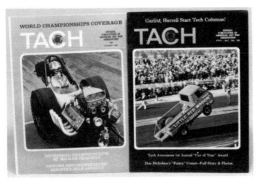

National Dragster, weekly publication, 1964 issues, each $2

Paperweight, "The Last Laps," Riverside, California, June 13–15, 1988, Chevy/Pontiac, new in box, $30

Pass, Indianapolis Motor Speedway, 1939, twenty-seventh race, $75

Pennant

San Jose Speedway, black felt shows 1950s roadster, rare, excellent condition, $50

William Grove Park and Speedway, 1950s, 16" long, green felt, $25

Pin

"Cummins Formula 300," brass color, figural diesel engine, copyright © 1979, $12

Jimmy Bryan Memorial/Dana 200, $10

National Hot Rod Association (NHRA), cloisonné, Member, 1987, $10

Target/Scotch Indy 500/Eddie Cheever, $10

Pinback Button

Great American Race, 10th Anniversary, wings with logo in center, $10

Monterey (California) Historic Auto Races, 1979, $8

Plate

Ceramic, 9", gold rim, center handpainted with

Tie, 1940s Indianapolis 500 souvenir, $40.

Hat pin, Drag Racing Videos, $3.

Hatpin, Jimmy Bryan, 200, 1986, $10.

Hat pin, Ernie Irvan, 1991 Daytona 500, $5.

Hat pin, Eddie Cheever, $5.

NHRA membership pin, 1987, $5.

Indianapolis 500 Plate, 1960s, $25.

Postcard, 1991 Great American Race, $3.

scenes from the Indianapolis 500, 1960s-era race car, flags and winged wheel logo in center, $25

Pewter, 6″, Indianapolis Motor Speedway, 1982 Collector Series, $35

Playing Cards, "The Great Race," double deck from Hallmark, nice print of 'teens racers, clear plastic case, $10

Postcard

Ford Benetton F1 Racing Team, $8

Indianapolis 500, shows Bobby Rahal driving Red Roof Inn/Cribari Wine Special, $10

Indianapolis Speedway, 1914, $15

Poster

Indianapolis 500, shows past winners and 1967 participants, very good condition, $50

Soap Box Derby Workshop/Clinic, 14″ by 22″ cardboard, 1967, $20

Print, Vanderbilt Race, recent reprint, nicely framed, $15

Program

Bonneville Speed Trials, 1974, autographed Jim Lattin, $15

Daytona Firecracker 400, July 4, 1963, Tiny Lund on cover, NASCAR sanctioned, $25

Detroit Grand Prix, 1984, $10

Gulf/Indy 500 playing cards, $25.

Poster, Miller/Rusty Wallace, $5.

NHRA Winternationals poster, hung in Chief Auto Parts Stores, $15.

East Coast Inaugural Championship Racing Program, Reading, Pennsylvania, Fairgrounds, March 28, 1954, $20

Indianapolis 500 First Race, 1922, good condition, loose covers, $1,500

Late Model Championship Stock Car Race, 1958, $20

Monroe, Michigan, 1952 NASCAR race, $25

Monterey (California) Historic Auto Races, 1979, $20

Record Album, *Sounds of the Drags*, AFX Comets, Fairlanes cover, $15

Program, 1963 Firecracker 400, Daytona, $25.

Indianapolis 500 program, 1976, $15.

Program, 1971 Carolina 500, $15.

Pennsylvania Pocono 500 program, 1971, $10.

Rule Book, American Hot Rod Association (defunct), 1970, $15

Ruler, American Racing Wheels, 12″ plastic ruler shows dragster and advertising, unusual, $20

Sheet Music, "Auto Race," cover artwork shows three cars, early teens, very rare, $50

Soda Bottle

Pepsi, Richard Petty Commemorative Tour, $5

Sun Drop soda, Dale Earnhart Collector Bottle, $5

Ticket, 1937 Indianapolis 500, $20

Ticket Order Form, flyer, 1965 Daytona 500, shows seating arrangements, race history, $5

Trophy, Long Island Auto Club Racing Trophy, 1909, $350

Trophy plate, Beeline Dragway, $5.

Program, USAC Race, 1958, $25.

Trophy, mounted 1961 Chevrolet, $25.

11

Tire Company Collectibles

Tire composition and size have changed drastically throughout the years. At first, vehicles had solid rubber tires. The earliest pneumatic tires were one piece, tire and tube together. This proved impractical, as whenever one wore out, tire and tube both had to be replaced. After 1900, the tire and tube were separated. This combination was used until the 1950s, when tubeless tires were introduced. Today, bias-ply tires have been replaced by radials.

Although few hobbyists collect tires, tire memorabilia is widely collected. As logos and signs changed throughout the years, they became collectible. One of the most well-remembered advertising characters is the Fisk boy, a charming child in a footed sleeper

License plate attachment, $25.

License plate attachment, Silvertown Tires, $40.

generally shown with a tire over one shoulder and holding a candle. This picture was usually shown with the slogan "Time to Re-tire." Another popular advertising figure is Mr. Bib, the Michelin Man. Collectors avidly seek out any items with his image on it—vinyl figures, plastic walkers, watches, and even playing cards.

Goodyear, best known for its blimp, used what hobbyists called the "winged foot" logo on many of its rubber products. Firestone's older logo was a stylized letter F in a shield.

Cornell Tires is not one of the best-known tire companies but its products are very collectible. Cornell tires were marketed through the Pep Boys chain of auto parts stores, and there are a lot of Pep Boys collectors who will purchase any and all Cornell memorabilia.

Tire companies produced many different advertising premiums incorporating a miniature tire. One of the most popular forms of tire advertising is the tire ashtray, currently experiencing a flurry of collector interest. A tire ashtray is just a miniature replica of a rubber tire embossed with a company name. These varied in size and tread design. Some of the early tire ashtrays had colored glass inserts embossed with spoked wheels common to 1920s automobiles. They contained a glass insert, usually embossed or painted with the manufacturer's name or local tire shop advertising, where the rim was supposed to be. All sorts of tire ashtrays were made, from the early 30 by 6.00 size bicycle-type tires to heavily ribbed tractor tires. Pin dishes were also made for the ladies, similar in size and design to the tire ashtray but without a flat area in which to lay a cigar or cigarette.

Some other advertising premiums incorporating miniature rubber tires were key chains, compasses, and tape measures. A few desk sets have been seen, such as a pen holder with a rubber tire base. Lamps were also made using a miniature rubber tire as a base.

The pen holder and the desk lamp are quite rare and were probably not widely distributed outside of the corporate headquarters.

Clocks were made as well. The earlier clocks were a key-wind variety before they went to electric. These are small clocks, often with an alarm. A Timex pocket watch has been seen with a rubber tire surround and the stem atop the tire. This is a very unusual item and may well have been an employee award of some sort.

When purchasing a rubber tire advertising piece, look for a tire that is soft and not cracked or dried out. Check ashtray inserts for chips and scratches. Clocks should be complete and, hopefully, in working order. The cost of repairing small key-wind or elec-

Federal tire postcard, space to stamp dealer's name, $10.

tric clocks often exceeds their value, so it's advisable to buy one that works.

Tire size is often embossed on the sides of these miniature rubber tires, and they can thus be approximately dated through these numbers. The tall, thin tires with sizes such as 30″ by 5″ or 32″ by 6″ were generally used on cars until the early 1930s. In the late 1930s, the heavier automobiles used 14″ and 15″ tires. The letter R in a series of numbers usually denotes radial and means your tire is recently made.

Other tire company advertising premiums, such as blotters, cigarette lighters, matchbooks, postcards, calendars, trays, and ice scrapers, are also collected.

A recent phenomenon is collector interest in tire company porcelain and tin signs. These colorful signs had taken a backseat to

Tire stand, B. F. Goodrich, tin, $35.

gas station and automobile dealer signs, but they are finally emerging as collectibles in their own right.

Tire company products are collectible as well, including tubes, patch kits, tire irons, tire pressure gauges, tire stands, and tire cut fillers. Old auto jacks and tire pumps are also great additions to a tire memorabilia collection.

Advertising Figure, Michelin Man, 14″ tall, vinyl, $60

Almanac, *1937 Goodrich Almanac for Farm and Home,* sixty-four pages, $15

Ashtray
  Brass, Co-Op Golden Tires, tire embossed in center, $25
  Cast iron, Co-Op Golden Tires, tire embossed in center, $25
  Glass, yellow/black, reads "1969 Industrial Product Sales Conference," Wingfoot logo, $15
  Tire Shape
    Armstrong Rhino-Flex, painted red and white, insert shows Rhino, $45
    Firestone, vinyl tire, red/white-painted glass, insert reads "I Love My Stones," 1960s, $25
    Firestone Safety Lock Cord, clear glass insert embossed with trylon and perisphere, 1939 New York World's Fair souvenir, $60
    General Balloon tire, embossed green glass insert reads "The General Tire Goes a Long Way to Make Friends," $45
    General Dual 90, yellow and orange enamel on clear glass insert, $25
    Goodyear, tractor tire, clear glass insert, $25

    Pennsylvania Tires, embossed blue glass insert, $45
    Pennsylvania Turnpike Tires, red/white-painted glass insert, $35
    U.S. Royal Master Air Ride, embossed glass insert, United States Rubber Company, $35
Atlas, Firestone, 1956, sixty-six pages, pocket travelogue and road atlas, $10

Ashtray, Rhino-Flex, rubber tire, $45.

Ashtray, Firestone, $25.

Badge, United States Rubber Products metal plant badge, embossed with tire and wreath, $35
Belt Buckle, Goodyear Blimp, copyright © 1974, $10
Blotter
Firestone Tires, shows 1920s roadster, unused, $8
Kelly-Springfield Heavy Duty Cord, shows tires and red bus, unused, $6
Book, *The Firestone Story,* Alfred Lief, 1951, 437 pages, forty-eight pages of photos, company history, $25
Booklet, *Firestone Tires,* souvenir of the 1933 Chicago World's Fair, $15
Cabinet, Bowes Seal Fast Tire Valves, 8″ by 9″ by 2″ deep tin cabinet with red and black Bowes logo, $35
Calendar, 1954 Royal Tires, pinup girls, $20

G&J Tires, blotter with 1920 calendar, $10.

Goodrich Route Book, 1915, $25.

Clock, Goodyear rubber tire on electric desk-size clock, $50
Cuff Links, Michelin Man, blue/white, 1960s, $35 pair
Flare Kit, Dayton Thorobred Tires, cardboard container, $5
Ice Scraper, 10″ long, Firestone Tires, red plastic, $3
Key Chain, tire shape, insert has advertisement for General Tires, Arizona dealer, $5
Lapel Pin
Goodyear Blimp, brass color, $15
Mellinger Tires, screw back, shows tire encircling globe, $20
Letterhead/Stationery, Kelly-Springfield, shows Miss Lotta Miles inside tire, reads "Keep Smiling with Kellys," $6

Lighter, General Tires, flat style, yellow plastic insert reads "The General Tire," $20

Map, Semperit Radials, map of Los Angeles, folds into pocket-size matchbook, $3

Medallion

"Fisk, Time to Re-Tire," 1938 brass medallion, embossed with Fisk boy with candle and tire, $35

General Dual-8, The World's Quickest Stopping Tire, aluminum coin, $15

Pencil, Mechanical

General Tire logo, Pennsylvania dealer, $15

Whitewall tires in oil-filled clear top, $35

Pin, Dayton-Walther Special, 3″ pinback, shows race car No. 77 and driver, $15

Plaque, Goodyear 1944 Quota Maker Contest, winged foot logo, 7″ by 9″, $45

Playing Cards

Michelin playing cards, single deck, shows Michelin Man, advertising in French, 1970s, $20

B. F. Goodrich ten year service pin, $25.

Michelin Man playing cards, $20.

Goodyear service pin, $20.

Playing cards, Patch-Rite for Safety, $30.

Patch-Rite for Safety, double deck, boxed, shows
   old tire and spoked rim, dated 1939, $30
Pump, 1930s metal hand pump, with oak handle,
   cloth-covered hose, $25
Sign
   B. F. Goodrich, tin sign, 17″ by 48″, $35
   General Tire, tin sign, $90

LEFT: Sign, Remington Tires, tin, $60.
RIGHT: Sign, Firestone Tires, porcelain, $125.

Goodyear Tire and Battery Service, tin, $75
Mohawk Tires, embossed tin, $50
U.S. Royal, shield-shaped tin, "Safety First,"
   $175
Tin
   Acme Valve Cores, 1″ by 2″ orange and blue
      tin, $5
   Fisk Anti-freeze, one-gallon can with boy with
      tire and candle logo, $35
   Fisk Radiator Flush, cone top, pictures boy with
      tire and candle logo, red/white/blue, $35
   Whiz Tyre-Wyte, "Makes black tires white," six-
      teen-ounce tin with Whiz logo, red/black/
      green, $25
Tire Cut Filler, Superior, yellow/red metal tube
   with metal lid, 1920s, unused with original box,
   $20
Tire Iron, G&J Tire Company, Indianapolis
   forged steel, 8½″ long, $20
Tire Pressure Gauge, made by Schraeder, en-
   graved with Fisk boy with tire and candle, reads
   "Time to Re-tire, Buy Fisk," $35

Tube repair kit, Allstate, tin, $12.

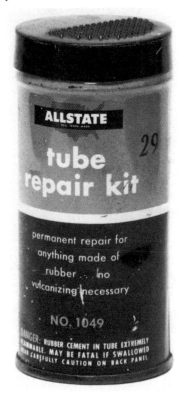

Tire patch kits, $10 each.

Tube repair kit, Camel, $10.

Tire Repair Patch Kits

   Allstate (Sears), tin, tube repair kit, $12
   Camel, cardboard oval, $10
   Monkey-Grip, colorful box, with apes, $10
   Oxford Tube Repair Kit, dated 1939, old cars on
      front of tin, $20

Tube repair kit, Electro Grip, $10.

Tube repair kit, Hold Tight, $12.

Speedpatch, tubeless tire patches, cardboard box, never opened, late 1950s, $10

Wizard (Western Auto) cardboard cylinder cold patch repair kit, $5

Tube, Fisk Air-Flight Deluxe Tube, cardboard box shows boy with tire and candle logo, $20

Tray, General Tires, 12″ diameter metal round tray shows 1927 Stutz Blackhawk Speedster, reads "Quality Tires since 1915," colorful, $35

Tray, General Tires, $25.

12

Truck and Commercial Vehicle Memorabilia

Fire truck, bus, taxi, military vehicle, and even recreational vehicle memorabilia is popular with truck and commercial vehicle collectors. Ambulances, hearses, delivery trucks, and tow trucks also have much to offer the truck history buff.

Members of police and fire departments often have an interest in restoring old emergency vehicles and collecting such paraphernalia. Bells, spotlights and sirens, and even polished brass fire extinguishers once mounted on an old fire truck are among the most desirable collectibles. Police badges, uniforms, caps, firefighters' helmets, boots, and fire trumpets are also collected. Perhaps the hottest truck collectible is toy fire trucks. There are many examples out there, from the larger pedal trucks to the pressed steel Smith-Miller trucks to the smallest Matchbox version. Toy fire trucks had a lot of small parts, such as hoses, ladders, and bells. Make sure all accessories are there before you buy.

Some famous names in American trucking history, such as Mack, Kenworth, and White, are still with us. Kenworth was founded in Washington State in 1923, manufacturing the heavy-duty logging trucks needed throughout the Pacific Northwest. Then the company branched out into making all kinds of trucks for local delivery needs as well as long-distance hauling.

Mack is well known for its famous bulldog

Kenworth 50th anniversary booklet, $15.

logo. There are hundreds of Mack collectibles available, from ashtrays with a chrome bulldog sitting in the center of it to a stuffed dog wearing a Mack collar.

Bus memorabilia collectors seem to favor Greyhound Bus Lines, perhaps because there is so much Greyhound memorabilia around. The bus depots offered many Greyhound souvenirs; toy buses, banks, and even salt and pepper shakers shaped like miniature blue and white buses are collected. These small cast-metal salt and pepper sets often have a decal on the roof that says "A souvenir of Pittsburgh" or some other city. The restaurant-style china used at bus depot cafeterias is also quite collectible. Most Greyhound dinnerware was ivory with a stripe around the rim and the famous running greyhound logo. This is usually stamped "Syracuse China" on the bottom. Silverware was stamped "Greyhound Bus Lines" on the handle. A complete place setting makes a nice display with other bus memorabilia. Trailways, Greyhound, and local bus line depot signs

are popular with collectors, with premium prices paid for the porcelain steel signs.

Bus drivers' uniforms and hat badges are often collected. Tie clips, cuff links, service pins, and other jewelry are desirable as well. Paper memorabilia is often sought out. Bus schedules are colorful and look good framed and displayed, as do older ticket stubs.

Taxi memorabilia is collectible as well. The word "taxi" usually brings to mind the sturdy, boxy Checker cabs so familiar on city streets. Drivers' caps, badges, and hack licenses are sought after, as are advertising and toy cabs.

Most automobile swap meets and shows look more like a motor home convention than an antique car meet, but few hobbyists stop to realize that the recreational vehicle (RV) is not a new idea. As early as 1913, a company displayed their "Motor Chapel," equipped with living accommodations for the pastor, at the Annual Exposition of Motor Trucks in Chicago. Model T motor homes are not uncommon, although most were hand built on a truck chassis by the owner. These early one-of-a-kind RVs did not offer all the luxuries of today's motor homes but most were well designed. In the 1930s, more and more companies were getting into the travel trailer business. Recreational traveling really was cut short by the restrictions of World War II; thus, the production of most RVs ceased. However, they experienced a revival in the 1960s, which led to the RV cult of today.

Pickups are by far the most popular of the trucks. Even new models are desired, often outselling automobiles. These light-duty trucks, or "Cowboy Cadillacs," are widely used throughout the country for daily transportation, household hauling, and even towing a boat or camp trailer. In short, Americans love their trucks.

Four-wheel drives have a special place in the hearts of collectors. International Scouts,

Greyhound Bus schedules, $5 each.

Ford's workhorse Broncos, and the Jeep are gaining respectability as collector vehicles. Consequently, the memorabilia from these rugged trucks has become more popular. Since World War II, the Jeep name has symbolized toughness and dependability. Jeep advertising leaned heavily on their service in the war, with these early ads often picturing a wartime bare-bones Jeep with a comparatively luxurious truck or station wagon. Now that the originals are gone—the full-size truck, the CJ5, the Jeepsters, and the Wagoneers— Jeep memorabilia, from advertising to toys to models to dealer signs, is sure to appreciate.

Truck memorabilia is as varied as automobilia. Many dealer sales brochures and catalogs have been reproduced as the older trucks have gained in their popularity with collectors. Original advertising is a little more difficult to find, however. Old farm magazines are a good place to start looking for old pickup ads. Truck collectibles can sometimes be found in unlikely places. Advertising premiums from other firms often pictured their delivery trucks. For example, a gasoline company advertising ashtray pictured an old tanker. A 1920s book from a paint store featured pictures of its fleet of Mack delivery trucks, and a deck of cards, obviously a Christmas gift for customers, shows a drawing of a dairy with a mid-1950s Chevrolet tanker out front.

Promotional truck models are even more unusual than automobile promos. There just were not as many produced. One of the very rarest is an early 1950s Chevrolet truck promo done by Jo-Han Plastics in 1958, which was actually a promotional item for B. F. Goodrich tire dealers. These tan and blue tow trucks with B. F. Goodrich–lettered tires enjoyed a short run of fifteen thousand. They are now very hard to find, and a near mint example would bring around $300.

Some of the newer truck promos are very well done and worth purchasing as an invest-

Robert Bosch Diesel Products clock with spark plug on right side (not shown), 1980s, $75.

ment. The 1988 Chevrolet pickup marked a comeback for pickup promotional models as it was their first pickup promo in fifteen years. Pickups were not as popular in the early 1970s as they are today, and Chevrolet discontinued truck promotional models. Ford has a new pickup promotional model that may be available from the dealer or from a promotional model dealer. It marks the fiftieth anniversary of the Ford pickup and sports a nice decal on the side.

Many super heavy-duty collector trucks are not practical for daily driving; thus, enthusiasts are delighted to find smaller souvenirs representing their favorite rig. Owners are always happy for a chance to get them out, shine them up, and show them off at club meetings, charity events, parades, and shows. You can't miss them at shows—big boys and girls behind the wheels of their giant-size toys, driving around the show area, offering rides to fellow club members and as many kids as they can squeeze onto the truck. Fire truck collectors too seem to enjoy driving their vehicles, cheerfully demonstrating lights, horns, and sirens.

Ashtray

Hennis Motor Freight, colorful truck in center of 6″ round, white ceramic ashtray, $10

Keith's Model T Truck Stop, glass, old truck painted in center, $5

Mack Bulldog, chrome figural dog on ashtray, $40

Badge

Cab driver, reads "Public Hack Driver, New York City, expires March 31, 1930," $25

Salesman's badge, 1968 Chevrolet golden anniversary trucks, heavy gold paper in plastic badge holder, reads "Job Tamer Trucks," $10

Teamsters Union, shows pre–World War II tractor-trailer, $20

Bell, brass, American La France Firetruck, $400

Belt Buckle, East Texas Motor Freight, early 1960s, $15

Blotter

Dodge panel truck, 1925, unused, $15

GMC Heavy Duty Trucks, 1951, unused, $5

Book, *American La France,* 1963–64 salesman's data book with original binder, $75

Bottle Opener, truck-shaped, reads "1st Million — Pontiac East," GMC plant, $12

Braclet, identification type, red cloisonné "Peterbilt" logo, $10

Brass Plate, 1920s Moller Taxi, $40

Bumper Sticker, vinyl, "I love my Chevy truck," $1

Button, "I LUV Chevy Trucks," $2

Calendar, 1979, Mack Bulldog desk calendar in envelope, $2

Cap, with visor, Yellow Cab, $135

Catalog

American Motors Police Cars, 1970, $15

Checker Cabs, 1961, $18

Ford Police Cars, 1953 models, $35

Studebaker Taxis, 1958, $20

Chauffeur's Badge

Arizona, 1933, $50

Colorado, 1920, $35

Illinois, 1948, $15

Indiana, 1933, $20

Kansas, undated, $45

Minnesota, 1940, $20

Paint store catalog showing delivery trucks, $10.

Blotter, professional cars, $10.

Blotter, Mack trucks, $10.

Chevrolet trucks, 1965, full line color catalog, $10.

Chauffeur's badge, 1925, New York, $25.

Chauffeur's badge, 1946, Ohio, $20.

Chauffeur's badge, 1954, Minnesota, $10.

Missouri, 1914, $125
New Mexico, 1938, $75
New York, 1917, $25
Oregon, 1923, $45
Texas, undated, $60

Coin
Chevy truck, 1937, Pikes Peak Hill Climb, bronze, $25
Dodge Trucks good-luck token, 1950s, $10

Cuff Links, Caterpillar, road grader, $20

Cup, United States Postal Service National Truck Maintenance Center, Norman, Oklahoma, Frankoma pottery, $5

Cup and Saucer, Greyhound Bus Lines, dog logo, Syracuse china restaurant ware, $15 each

Desk Set, 1950s Truck Salesman, NOS, $50

Fire Extinguisher
American La France, dated 1964, 3″ diameter, 14″ long, white metal with bracket, $20
Brass, black painted steel mounting bracket, $95

First-Aid Kit, plastic case, 1972 Chevrolet Trucks, Iowa dealer, unusual, $20

Key Chain
Diamond T–Willys trucks, $15
Dodge/Indy 500 Pace Truck, 1987, $5
Dodge Trucks, 1960s-style flower, plastic, $5

Light, dealer showroom item, reads "GMC the truck people" on plastic shade, wooden base, 1968–70s era, $35

Lighter
Figural oil drum, Dodge trucks, 1950s, $45
Fruehauf Roadster miniature trailer encased in Lucite, chrome lighter in top, $20

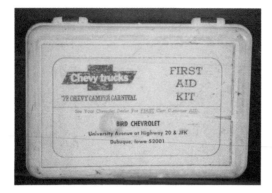

Chevrolet Truck first aid kit, 1972, $20.

Greyhound Lines bus first aid kit, $50.

GMC, truck light, $35.

Liquor Decanter, ceramic, Old Mr. Boston,
  Firetruck, No. 24, Spirit of '76, $25
Matchbook
  Holdan Corporation, Georgia, shows 1957
    Chevrolet trucks with utility beds, $3
  Roadway Express tractor-trailer, $1
Money Clip
  Brass, "Clip your costs with Mack Trucks,"
    shows truck, $125
  GMC, gold/black cloisonné, $10
Mug
  Alemund Volunteer Fire Department, 50th An-
    niversary, 1935–85, shows Russell Steam En-
    gine, $10
  Shows 1929 Chevrolet stake-bed truck, bottom
    stamped "1961 Truck Sales Honor Club,"
    $25
Notepad, Chevrolet Truck Sales Professional, $10
Nozzle, brass, embossed Packard Firetrucks, $75
Paperweight
  Ambulance service, Texas, contains picture of
    'teens ambulance, $45

Red flashing light, $75.

Ford, Southwest Truck Conference, Lucite, $6

Pencil, wooden, ½″ diameter, shows 1955 Chevrolet truck emblem, reads "Task Force Trucks," $5

Penknife

Chrome, Chevy Task Force Trucks, $20

Swiss Army style, reads "Ford Trucks," leather case, $15

Pin, Two Year Safe Driver, Yellow Cab, gold color, $40

Pinback Button, 2½″ diameter, pre–World War II, "Switch to Dodge Trucks and Save Money," $25

Playing Cards

Chicago Firefighters Union logo, 1950s, used, complete deck, $6

"GMC Truck," newer issue, year unmarked, $5

Hawthorne-Mellody Dairy, Wisconsin, shows late 1950s Chevrolet milk tanker, sealed, $10

Robertson Motor Freight, shows 1940s Kenworth, gold deck, sealed, $15

Postcard

Bronco, 1967, $4

Chevrolet pickup, 1956, $5

Poster, 1943, color, 19″ by 22″, Coast Guard with Jeeps, $65

Playing cards with milk tanker, $10.

Mack pin, $15.

Postcard, issued by Jeep dealer, $8.

Robertson Motor Freight playing cards, $15.

Postcard, 1940s, military trucks, $6.

Promotional Model, 1993 Chevrolet Suburban, "Indianapolis 500 Official Truck," $30

Tray, Mack Trucks, 1900–1959, gold color, shows many old Macks, $75

Ring, Ford Truck Sales Workshop, sterling, $125

Ruler

Tin, 12″, York Moving, shows 1950s Allied Van, $10

Wooden, 12″, Dodge/Plymouth Job Rated Trucks, $6

Service Pin

Bekins, five year, screw back, $30

City Lines (local bus company), 10 karat solid-gold pin, red stone, $35

Dependable, one year, Safe Driver pin, Greyhound Lines, $25

Diebold service pin, $10.

Diebold Trucking, ten-year pin, sterling, $10

Shoe Brush, advertisement for casket company, shows 1920s hearse on back of brush, $20

Sign

Greyhound, oval porcelain, dog logo, $750

"Merrick Scale Manufacturing Co," porcelain, 4″ by 20″, from truck scale, $25

National Trailways System, Bus Depot, porcelain, $500

Spoon, Greyhound Bus Lines, $25

Thermometer

Tin, 9″ long, Caterpillar advertising, $20

White enamel on metal, 4″ by 12″, "Nationwide Horse Transportation," shows mid-1920s Ford truck, $15

Tie Bar

Dodge Builds Tough Trucks, $10

Ford Truck Workshop, black/gold, older-style split tie bar, $20

Greyhound, souvenir of the 1939 World's Fair, $20

Reads "Mack," with bulldog, $15

Shows International Scout, gold color, $10

Tie Tack, Chevy Police Package, blue/gold, $10

Timetable, Greyhound Bus Lines, 1946, $10

Tool Check, Mack Plant, aluminum coin, $5

Trading Card, *Truckin' Magazine*, 1973, series of forty-four, $.25

Vase, ceramic, shows 1980 Ford pickup, logo of North Dakota dealer, $5

Watchband Calendar, monthly metal calendar wraps around watchband, salesman's item, mounted on cards with tips for selling Chevrolet trucks, May 1971, $3

13

Toys

Toy cars have been around as long as the automobile. Since the first automobile enthusiast carved a likeness of a horseless carriage out of wood, collecting toy cars has been almost as popular as collecting the vehicles themselves.

When you attend a local toy show one day and then an antique car swap meet the next, you will see lots of familiar faces among the swappers and the shoppers. The vendors come because they know that old-car people love old toy cars almost as much as the real thing. The swappers come to look over the collectible automobiles, to buy parts and accessories for their favorite old car, and to buy toys representing that car.

Many are specialists, collecting toys that mirror their interests in the hobby. A Chrysler Airflow owner may buy only Airflow toys. Other collectors may want only a certain type of toy, looking for fire trucks, taxis, or buses.

The most popular collector cars are often the most popular toys. The 1957 Chevrolet has long been considered one of the most sought after collector cars, and a recent sur-

Korris Kars, Corvette & Mako Shark, $35.

vey found that replicas of the 1957 Chevrolet automobile were the top-selling die-cast toy cars. Chevrolet produced millions of cars in 1957 and they are not rare, but everyone seems to fondly remember one owned by a friend or relative.

Some collectors actually prefer collecting toys to the real automobiles because they can afford more of them, they have enough room to display their treasures, and they don't cost anything to keep up.

Automobile hobbyists are enthusiastic collectors of dealer promotional model cars. These are thought to have begun in 1932 when Graham-Paige authorized Tootsietoy to produced a four-inch-long replica of its new vehicles. Many of these were boxed and handed out in the Graham showrooms. After World War II, the distribution of quarter-scale promotional models became more common. These were actually designed with the cooperation of the automakers and were authentically detailed. At first, models by Product Miniatures, National Products, and Aluminum Model Toys (later to become AMT) were cast metal. They were usually painted and some were made into banks. It was common to have the local dealer's name and address printed on the model car. In the 1950s,

promotional model makers turned to plastic, which was cheaper than metal and the color could be molded in, eliminating the need for painting. These were even more realistic, with clear windows and interior details that matched the real thing. A good promotional model should be easily recognized as the make, model, and year it is intended to represent. The year of manufacture is often embossed in the rear license plate area, and some promos have features embossed on the undercarriage as well. Some of the plastic promos also contain an AM radio in lieu of an interior. These are more unusual than the regular promo but are not as desirable.

Promotional model car prices vary widely, depending on the rarity and popularity of the automobile itself. Corvette promotional models are quite expensive. A quarter-scale dealer promotional model of the 1963 Split Window Stingray is close to $1,000 for a mint version. Mustang promotional models are also very popular, with the rarer high-performance models being most desirable. Models of some of the new cars can be purchased from the dealers for around $20. When shopping for promos, be sure all the small chrome parts are present and check for the warping that is so common in plastic products of the 1950s. Some of the Jo-Han models of the 1950s and 1960s are currently available as reissues. Chevrolet has also released replicas of some of its older Corvette promos.

Model car kits are popular as well. These were available in a variety of scales and materials. Some hobbyists enjoy building the kits while others place a premium on kits that are unopened or unbuilt. Whether you want to build the kit or not, buying an unbuilt model car kit is the best way to be sure all the small parts are there. The first model car kits were of balsa wood and required a great deal of skill to assemble. In 1951, Revell offered the first plastic model kit, a Maxwell in what was

Plastic gas tanker, MIB, $20.

called their "Old Timers" series. Plastic kits gave us more choices of color, details, and chrome accessories. Scales ranged from HO to the larger one-twelfth, with the one-quarter version being the most popular. AMT's "3 in 1" series kits gave the model builder a choice of building a car that was factory stock, a drag racer, or a low 'n' slow custom. Metal models were available as well. The Hubley dies have been acquired by JLE Scale Models and the metal Ford Model A kits are again available. Many of the popular model kits are being re-issued, such as the Monkeemobile-cus-tomized GTO.

For many automotive toy collectors, the pedal car is the ultimate toy. The first riding toys were hand-crafted miniature cars made by talented fathers for their children. Soon they were mass-produced in pressed steel by such makers as Keystone and National. The cheaper models consisted of a basic metal body, with pedal mechanism or chain drive. For the more affluent children, however, there were remarkably realistic pedal cars, representing the finer automobiles of the day. Luxury appointments, such as comfortable upholstery rather than a metal seat, operating horns and lights, and fancy pinstriping, make the more elaborate pedal cars very collectible today. It seems that almost every month a beautifully restored pedal car reaches another record price at auctions and sales. In some cases, it seems the pedal car prices have surpassed those of some of the actual automobiles of the era.

There is also a lot of collector interest in the postwar Japanese tin toy cars, particularly those that represent an American car of the era. Many Japanese tin toy cars are a generic sort of vehicle, which could represent almost any make, but some toy auto manufacturers designed their tin toys so well that they are easily identified. Bandai is known for its well-detailed tin cars. Original boxes add a lot to the value of any collectible, and it is espe-cially true with Japanese tin toy cars. Their boxes were very colorful and imaginative, although they seldom matched the toy inside. Some of the Japanese tin toy cars run on friction motors but many are battery-operated.

Toy race cars are high up on the wish lists of collectors today. Gas-powered versions with such names as McCoy, Thimbledrome, Dooling, and Ohlson-Rice are so desirable that their prices are escalating beyond the reach of many collectors. If gas-powered cars are your area of interest, look at some of the Cox plastic cars of the 1960s. The Corvette and the Dune Buggy are two very nice models equipped with the peppy .049 Thimbledrome motor. These are still reasonably priced and easier to find that some of the earlier models. These little cars are so much fun to race that some radio-control hobbyists are returning to the older gas-powered vehicles for racing.

Interest is increasing in some of the early remote-control cars as well, especially some

Racing Champions/Cale Yarborough, $10.

Andy Gard telephone truck, $100.

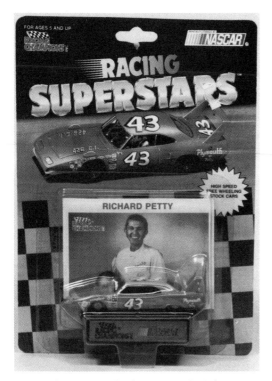

Racing Champions/Richard Petty Superbird, $10.

of the 1950s and 1960s cars by such makers as Irwin and Andy Gard and countless Japanese toy makers. These toy plastic cars with the wire leading to a hand-held battery box with controls were the pioneers of today's radio-controlled cars. Only a few collectors find these of interest just yet, so they are still af-

Futuristic car, Irwin Plastics, $95.

fordable and sure to appreciate in value. Some of the models made in the 1950s were replicas of the streamlined, futuristic vehicles seen at car shows at that time.

Slot car racing sets were so popular in the 1960s that they very nearly put the electric train makers out of business. The cars represented some of the most exotic race cars of the day, including the Chaparral, the Cheetah, and the Cobra. Almost everyone got into the act — Lionel, Gilbert, Marx, Revell, Cox, Strombecker, and Eldon are just a few manufacturers of slot car sets. Aurora made HO-scale racing legendary with its Thunderjets of the early 1960s. It offered Mustangs, Fairlanes, Galaxies, and Buick Rivieras, along with such customized cars as the original Batmobile and the Green Hornet Lincoln.

Hot Wheels are the 1957 Chevrolet of the toy collecting world. They, like the 1957 Chevy, were produced in large quantities but are still extremely popular with collectors. Hot Wheels were started in 1968 by Mattell Toy Company in California. Many were hot rods, souped-up versions of the street machines of the time. They were also imaginatively named. The Cougar was called Nitty Gritty Kitty and the ever-popular 1955 Chevrolet Nomad was called Alive 55. These diecast miniature cars came with doors and hoods that opened and with huge motors. They had hot metallic paint, flames, and lots

Texaco airport tanker, $95.

of small chromed plastic parts. They even had the redline tires offered on high-performance cars in the 1970s. Best of all, they were cheap. At less than $1 new, almost every interested kid in the 1960s and 1970s had a nice selection of Hot Wheels. The most collectible vehicles are those still in blister packs.

Hot Wheels really hurt Matchbox sales. Matchbox had been exporting toy cars to the United States since the early 1950s. Its cars came in the familiar blue and yellow boxes. The models that represented American cars were fairly plain compared to the California-style street rods Hot Wheels was producing. Matchbox offered a mundane Mercury station wagon, a 1960s Ford Fairlane police car, and a Plymouth fire chief car in its numbered—one to seventy-five—regular wheels series. One of the rarer early Matchbox series American cars is the yellow 1964 Chevrolet four-door sedan with gray wheels and taxi decals. To try to recapture the market from Hot Wheels and its distinctive custom cars, Matchbox converted to Superfast Wheels and offered more modified automobiles in brighter colors. Although Matchbox models are still available, the most appealing to collectors are those with their original boxes that were made in England by Lesney.

Ertl Company has been famous for some time for its scale-model farm toys, but automobile toy collectors know it best for its line of collectible banks. Since the 1980s, Ertl has produced almost two thousand automobile and truck replica banks with many different advertising logos. These are generally on a quarter scale, and oil company advertising is among the most popular with collectors. There are many variations as to body style, paint color, and kinds of wheels and tires used, so it is best to do your homework before collecting the banks. At this time, Ertl has announced plans to discontinue the 1950 Chevrolet panel truck bank; thus, these are expected to go up in price. There are good price guides to the Ertl banks available, and they are quite helpful in determining the numbers produced along with the current values.

Exotic toy cars, especially die-cast replicas and scale models—kits made by some of the excellent customizing wizards of the 1950s, 1960s, and 1970s—are highly sought after by toy car collectors. Tom Daniel's "S'cool bus," a yellow high-performance model guaranteed to get you to school on time, is an all-time favorite in either the model kit or the die-cast Hot Wheels version.

Toys have been the hot item in the collectibles market for some time. Unfortunately, as desirability increased so have the prices. Old toys are no longer just hand-me-downs saved for the grandkids; they are an investment.

Amos and Andy Car, tin windup (currently being reproduced), $800
Auburn Rubber
1935, Ford coupe, 4″ long, $30
1946, Lincoln convertible, 4½″ long, $25
1937, Oldsmobile, 4 door sedan, 4½″, $25

Banks, Ertl Company
Antique Auto Club of America, Fall 1991 Meet, bank is a 1926 Seagrave Firetruck, only 504 made, $30
Check the Oil, IPCA No. 1, 1937 Ford tanker, 540 made, red/white, $55

Castrol bank, Ertl, $40.

Lincoln Bank, Banthrico, $15.

Classic Motorbooks, 1990, 25th Anniversary,
    1950 Chevrolet panel truck bank, only 4,524
    produced, blue/silver, $35
Gulf Refining, 1950 Chevrolet panel, 1984, only
    311 made, $2,500
Harley-Davidson, No. 1, 1918 Runabout, 1988,
    5,088 made, $400
Texaco, No. 2, 1926 Mack Tanker, 5,000 made
    in 1985, $425
Barbie, 1957 Chevrolet convertible, blue plastic,
    MIB, $75
Barclay, 1937 Chevrolet sedan, slushcast, marked
    only "Made USA," orange/gray with white rub-
    ber tires, 4″ long, $45
Board Games
    Auto Race Game, Milton Bradley, 1925, $200

Barclay 1939 Chevrolet, $40.

Calling All Cars, Parker Bros., 1938, $75
Champion Spark Plug Road Race, advertising
    premium game, $35
Drag Racing Game, only available with mail
    away offer from Plymouth, Day Publishing,
    1968, $95
Let's Take a Trip, 1962, Milton Bradley, $25

Standard Oil checkers, $60.

Let's Take a Trip, board game, $25.

Speed Circuit, board game, $10.

Midget Auto Race, Cracker Jack Co., 1930, $25

Touring, card game, Parker Bros., 1926, $60

Buddy L

Army Signal Corps Truck, 1942, 12″ long, $250

Model T Ford Flivver Roadster, 1925–27, $1,000

Riding Academy Truck, 1958, 12″ long, $200

Bus

Greyhound, realistic, $150

Kenton, cast iron, 6″ long, double-decker, 1920s, $800

Candy Container, 1940s, Jeep, 4″ long, $40

Cast Iron

AC Williams, coupe with rumble seat, 6″, $195

Arcade, stake truck, $400

Kingsbury Airflow, green, restored, $300

Chrysler Airflow

Hubley, cast iron, 1930s, 4½″ long, $200

Pressed steel, 1937, 6″ long, $100

Cleveland Toy, aluminum racing car, 1935, 13″, $350

Courtland, Fire Chief Car, friction, 7″ long, $90

Dick Tracy Copmobile, Ideal, $125

Dinky

Cadillac Ambulance, 1965, near mint, no box, $45

Ford Thunderbird, #106, two passenger, MIB, $85

Lincoln Zephyr, #39, MIB, $300

Plymouth, 1963, #137, MIB, $35

Plymouth Station Wagon, #27, 1948, MIB, $125

Pontiac, 1968, #252, MIB, $45

Doepke Model Toys, American La France Fire Pumper, 18″, $350

Electric Automobile, 1903, made by Knapp, 11″ long, pressed steel, 1903, battery operated, rare, $4,000

Erie Cars (Parker White Metal)

Lincoln Zephyr sedan, 1936, 3½″ long, $50

Packard Roadster, 1936, 6″ long, $75

F&F Plastic Cars, promotional items given as premiums in Post cereals from 1955–1964

Ford Fire Chief Car, 1956, $18

Mustang Coupe, 1964, (currently reproduced), $4

Plymouth Station Wagon, 1958, $12

Game, *Whee-Whiz*, Marx Auto Race Game, tin windup, $500

Gas-Powered Cars

Cox Corvette, 1964, red, Thimbledrome Motor, $125

Cox Dune Buggy, Thimbledrome Motor, MIB, $95

Ohlsson & Rice midget race car, aluminum body, rubber tires, 1940s, $600

Testor's Sprite, red/white, MIB, $95

Thimbledrome Racer, #20, $325

Thimbledrome Racer, #25, red/blue, $275

Thimbledrome Racer, #40, yellow/blue, $300

Thimbledrome Racer, #45, near mint, $400

Gas Station

Gibbs gas station, tin/wood/paper, $350

Marx Sunnyside tin gas station, $400

Gilmore Special, gas powered, $2,500.

Dinky Rambler station wagon, $35.

F&F Ford/Post cereal premium, $15.

Superior Service Station, Marx, $125.

Hot Wheels Fire Chief, MIP, $45.

Hess, promotional models from Hess gasoline stations, sold each year during the Christmas season
  B-Model Mack Tanker, 1964, MIB, first issue, $1,200
  Box trailer with barrels, 1976, MIB, $200
  Fire Truck with ladders, 1989, MIB, $35
Hot Wheels
  Ambulance, 1970, Heavyweights, redline tires, near mint, $25
  Custom El Dorado, 1968, redline tires, lime green, near mint, $25
  Custom Fleetside, pickup, purple, redline tires, near mint but no blister pack, $35
  Paddy Wagon, 1993, blue, Mint in Package, redline tires, a Hot Wheels 25th Anniversary reissue, $5
  Red Baron, 1969, redline tires, mint in blister pack, $50
  S'Cool Bus, 1971, Mint in Package, redline tires, $200
Hubley
  Auto carrier, repaint, $65
  Log truck, 9″, MIB, $100
Ideal
  Ford Pickup Truck, 1940, 4″ plastic, $35

Hubley Duesenberg metal model, $90.

Hess truck, 1977, tanker, $125.

"Take Apart Cadillac," 1956, 12", blue plastic with tools, MIB, $150

Japanese Tin Toy Cars

Buick Roadmaster, 1955, 11" long, friction, $350

Cadillac, T.N., 1952, battery operated, 13½", $350

Chevrolet Ambulance, 1958, 8", Bandai, $250

Oldsmobile Toronado, 1966, battery operated, red coupe, $75

Plymouth Station Wagon, 1958, friction, Bandai, blue/white, $150

Kilgore, cast iron Pierce Arrow Roadster, 6" long, $500

Manoil, 1950s plastic roadster, 4" long, $10

Marx

Coca Cola advertising truck, pressed steel, 10" long, Sprite Boy decal, $250

"Fanny Farmer," plastic advertising truck, $60

Jeep, 1940s, 11" long, $150

Jumping Jeep, Marx tin windup, $250

Matchbox

#1, Dodge Challenger, Superfast Wheels, MIB, 1976, $7

#4, Pontiac Firebird, Superfast Wheels, MIB, $15

#4, '57 Chevy, Superfast Wheels, MIB, 1981, $5

#6, Ford Pickup, 1969, $12

#8, Ford Mustang Fastback, MIB, 1966, $25

#9, Javelin, 1972, $15

#20, Chevrolet Taxi, yellow, gray wheels, MIB, $200

#22, Pontiac Grand Prix, 1964, $25

#54, Cadillac Ambulance, white, excellent, no box, regular wheels, $15

#66, Greyhound Bus, regular wheels, near mint, no box, $15

#73, Mercury Station Wagon, lime, very good, no box, regular wheels, $10

Nash Metropolitan, 1955, $50

Rambler American, 1962, $20

Model Car Kits

AMT, 1932 Ford Roadster, "3 in 1" kit, unbuilt, $60

AMT, 1959 Corvette, "3 in 1," unbuilt, $125

Jo-han, 1970 Rebel Machine, unbuilt, $75

Bandai, 1958 Plymouth, $150.

Model, Pontiac Club De Mer, built, $35.

Battery operated Toronado, $75.

MPC 1969 Chevrolet truck model kit, built, $20.

Monogram, 1966 Mustang, GT350, factory
sealed, $75

MPC, 1969 Dodge Coronet, "Mission Impossible," factory sealed, $275

Motorcycle

Harley Davidson, Hubley cast-iron with side car
and rider, $1,500

Harley Davidson, Matchbox Limited Edition,
1992, boxed set of four motorcycles and
poster, $35

Nylint

American Oil Emergency Truck, 11", 1963,
$125

Ford Bronco, 1966, 12" long, $175

Ford Speedway Truck with Race Car, 1952, 25"
long, $225

Paper Cut Out, Army Ambulance, Handicraft,
1942, uncut, $40

Pedal Car

AMF Firetruck with ladders, 1970, $150

Buick, late 1920s, Steelcraft, 36" long, $3,000

Cadillac, 1915, Toledo Metal Wheel Company,
litho dash, $1,500

Chain drive, 1905, wooden spoke wheels,
$2,500

Chrysler Airflow, $1,200

Early open coupe, 1920s, 36" long, Glendron,
$400

Firetruck, American National hose reel truck, restored, $7,500

Ford, emblem on radiator, $800

Hudson, folding windshield, $800

Lincoln, by Gendron, $3,000

Mack Firetruck, Steelcraft, $800

Mercer Raceabout, 1920, $4,000

Nash, 1920s, 34" long, $2,500

Packard dual cowl phaeton, 6' long, American
National, $6,000

Packard Roadster, 1920s, 45" long, American
National, $2,600

Pioneer, race car, metal and wood, $1,500

Winner, 1906, $2,000

Promotional Models

Chevrolet convertible, 1960, $125

Chevrolet station wagon, 1956, $115

Corvair, 1966, red coupe, $200

Corvette coupe, 1967, blue, $1,500

Corvette coupe/split window, 1963, $800

Edsel Hardtop, 1958, pink, $250

Metropolitan promotional model, $175.

Mustang 1964 1/2 promotional model with box, $200.

Fairlane, 1966, $100

Ford, 1958, $125

GTO, 1967, red, MIB, $400

Hudson, 1951, $90

Impala, 1963, turquoise, MIB, $250

Mustang, 1964½, MIB, $200

Oldsmobile 442, 1969, green, $95

Riviera, 1967, radio promo, $60

Thunderbird convertible, 1964, $75

Pyro Plastic, U.S. Army truck, 3" long, olive drab,
$10

Remote Control, 1953 Pontiac, gray plastic, MIB,
$125

Renwal, plastic Cadillac, 5½" long, $25

Roadster, pressed steel, wooden wheels, possibly
Marx or Wyandotte (unmarked), 1930s, approx.
8" long, $125

Slot Cars

Ideal Motorific Torture Track, four cars, MIB,
$150

VIP Raceways slot car, early 1960s Indy-type car,
MB, $75

Smith Miller (Smitty Toys)

"B" Mack, PIE, 18 wheeler, $700

GMC Heinz Grocery Truck, Stakebed, $400

Structo, Bearcat Racer, 12" long, clockwork, $700

Sun Rubber, 4 door 1940s Dodge sedan, good
condition, $25

Sun Rubber Sedan, fair condition, $10

Tonka

  Ford tow truck, 1956, red/white, 12″ long, $250

  Jeep Stakebed Truck, 1964, 9½″ long, $60

Tootsietoy

  American LaFrance fire truck, 1954, near mint, 3″, $15

  Buick Roadster, 1926, $85

  Ford Falcon, 1960, 3″, $15

  Ford Model T open touring car, metal wheels, 1915–26, $75

  Jeepster, 1947, 3″, $30

  La Salle coupe, 1930s, white rubber tires, $200

Winross

  Howard Johnson semitruck, MIB, $165

  Sunoco truck, $50

Wyandotte, Chrysler Town and Country woodie convertible, 1940s, 12″ long, top goes up and down, $300

Directory of Clubs, Museums, and Publications

American Truck Historical Society, 300 Office Park Drive, Birmingham, AL 35223

Antique Automobile Club of America, 501 W. Governor Road, P.O. Box 417, Hershey, PA 17033 (sponsor of the famous Fall Hershey Meet)

Antique Motorcycle Club of America, Box 333, Sweetser, IN 46987

Antique Toy World, P.O. Box 34509, Chicago, IL 60634

Auto Racing Memories, P.O. Box 12226, Saint Petersburg, FL 33733

Automobile Objects d'Art Club, 252 N. Seventh Street, Allentown, PA 18102

Automobilia News (newsletter), P.O. Box 3528, Glendale, AZ 85311

Automotive Modelers Society, 806 S. Ripley, Neosho, MO 64850

Contemporary Historical Vehicle Association, 16944 Dearborn Street, Sepulveda, CA 91343

Gilmore—Classic Car Club of America Museum, 6865 Hickory Road, Hickory Corners, MI 49060

Horseless Carriage Club of America, 128 S. Cypress Street, Orange, CA 92666

Indianapolis Motor Speedway Museum, 4790 W. Sixteenth Street, Indianapolis, IN 46222

International Petroliana Collector's Association, Drawer 1000, Westerville, OH 43081

Light Commercial Vehicle Association, 316 Berkley Court, Jonesboro, TN 37659

Military Vehicle Preservation Association, P.O. Box 260607, Lakewood, CO 80226

Mini License Plate/Keychain Tag Collectors, c/o Dr. Miles, 888 Eighth Avenue, New York, NY 10019

Mobilia (newsletter), P.O. Box 575, Middlebury, VT 05753

Model A Ford Club of America, 250 S. Cypress, La Habra, CA 90631

Model T Ford Club of America, Box 7400, Burbank, CA 91510

Mustang Club of America, Box 447, Lithonia, GA 30058

National Automobile Museum, 10 Lake Street South, Reno, NV 89501

Nostalgia Drag Racing Association, P.O. Box 9438, Anaheim, CA 92802

Pate Museum of Transportation, P.O. Box 711, Pate, TX 76101 (known for its huge swap meet every April)

Quartermilestones (Drag Racing Memorabilia Collector's Newsletter), c/o Geoff Stunkard, Oxhaven Apartments, Apt. C-38, Oxford, PA 19363

Redline (Hot Wheels Collector Club), 2263 Grahan Drive, Santa Rosa, CA 95404

Society for the Preservation and Appreciation of Motor Fire Apparatus in America, P.O. Box 2005, Syracuse, NY 13320

The Society of Automotive Historians, c/o The National Automotive History Collection, Detroit Public Library, 5201 Woodward Avenue, Detroit, MI 48202

Towe Ford Museum, 2200 Front Street, Sacramento, CA 95818

U.S. Toy Collector, P.O. Box 4244, Missoula, MT 59806

Veteran Motor Car Club of America, P.O. Box 360788, Strongsville, OH 44136

Vintage Chevrolet Club of America, P.O. Box 5387, Orange, CA 94667

World Organization of Automotive Hobbyists, P.O. Box 1331, Palm Desert, CA 92261

Bibliography

BOOKS

Anderson, Scott. *Check the Oil.* Radnor, Pa.: Wallace-Homestead Book Company, 1986.

Bloemker, Al. *Five Hundred Miles to Go.* Coward-McCann, 1961.

Burness, Tad. *Cars of the Early Thirties.* New York: Galahad Books by arrangement with Chilton Book Company, Radnor, Pa., 1970.

Butterworth, W. E. *An Album of Automobile Racing.* Chicago: Franklin Watts Publishing, 1977.

Gunnell, John. *Chevrolet Pickups, 1946–72.* Motorbooks International, 1988.

Clymer, Floyd. *Those Wonderful Old Automobiles.* Bonanza Books, 1953.

Gabbard, Alex. *Vintage and Historic Racing Cars.* Los Angeles: HP Books, 1986.

Georgana, G. N., ed. *Encyclopedia of American Automobiles.* New York: E. P. Dutton, 1968.

Georgana, G. N., and Carlo Demand. *Trucks, An Illustrated History, 1986–1920.* Two Continents Publishing Group, 1978.

Hertz, Louis. *The Complete Book of Building and Collecting Model Automobiles.* New York: Crown Publishing, 1970.

Huxford, Sharon, and Bob Huxford, eds. *Schroeder's Antiques Price Guide, 8th ed.* Paducah, Ky.: Collector Books, 1990.

Kimes, Beverly Rae, ed. *Complete Handbook of Automobile Hobbies.* Kutztown, Pa.: Automobile Quarterly Publications, 1981.

Martells, Jack. *Antique Automobile Collectibles.* Chicago: Contemporary Books, 1980.

Partridge, Bellamy. *Fill 'er Up.* New York: McGraw-Hill, 1952.

Rinker, Harry, ed. *Warman's Americana, 5th ed.* Radnor, Pa.: Wallace-Homestead Book Company, 1991.

Sears, Stephen W. *The American Heritage History of the Automobile in America.* Boston: American Heritage Publishing, 1977.

Smith, Jack H. *Postcard Companion.* Radnor, Pa.: Wallace-Homestead Book Company, 1989.

Smith, Mark, and Naomi Black. *America on Wheels.* New York: William Morrow, 1986.

Stein, Ralph. *The Treasury of the Automobile.* Racine, Wis.: Golden Press, 1961.

Wherry, Joseph. *Automobiles of the World.* New York: Galahad Books, 1968.

Zolomij, John J. *The Motorcar in Art.* Kutztown, Pa.: Automobile Quarterly Publications, 1990.

PERIODICALS

Hemmings' Vintage Auto Almanac, 9th ed. (1992).
Heuser's Quarterly Price Guide to Official Collectible Banks (July–September 1992).
Hot Rod Magazine (January 1990).
Jay Ketelle's Wish Book (1991 and 1992).

Russell, Joseph. *Automobilia Sales List* (1991 and 1992).
Stunkard, Geoff. *Quarter Milestones, Drag Racing Memorabilia Newsletter,* 1 and 2.
Wherry, Joseph. "Antique and Classic Cars," *Trend Magazine* 193 (1960).

Subject Index

Index to Companies and Clubs